The Ness Fireside Book
of
GOD GHOSTS GHOULS
And other true stories

Lachlan Ness

Akangarooloose

The Ness Fireside Book of God Ghosts Ghouls...

By the same author:
A Kangaroo Loose in the Top Paddock
A Kangaroo Loose in Shetland
One Memorable Summer

© 2013 Lachlan Ness

All rights reserved. No part of this book may reproduced, in whole or in part, by any means including photocopying or any other information storage and retrieval system, without the written consent of the author.

Scripture taken from THE HOLY BIBLE, NEW INTERNATIONAL VERSION®. Copyright (c) 1973, 1978, 1984 by International Bible Society. Used by permission of Zondervan Publishing House. All rights reserved.
The 'NIV' and 'New International Version' trademarks are registered in the United States Patent and Trademark Office by International Bible Society. Use of either trademark requires the permission of International Bible Society.

National Library of Australia Cataloguing-in-Publication entry

Author: Ness, Lachlan, author.

Title: The Ness fireside book of God ghosts ghouls
            and other true stories / Lachlan Ness.

ISBN: 9780987408433 (paperback)

Subjects: Faith.
            Belief and doubt.
            Ghost stories.
            Christian philosophy.

Dewey Number: 234.23

Published by Akangarooloose.com
Typesetting by Bill Lang
Cover by Helen Marshall
Printed by CreateSpace

... and other true stories

CONTENTS

Acknowledgements		v
'Welcome to 'Puddleby on Sea'		1
My own earliest story; a supernatural incident		4
1	GHOSTS	8
2	HAUNTINGS	32
3	VISITATIONS	46
4	UNEXPLAINABLE, INEXPLICABLE	55
5	PREMONITIONS	72
6	'LET THE CHILDREN COME TO ME'	99
7	STRANGE LIGHTS AND OTHER MYSTERIES	107
8	THE MATTER OF EVIL	115
9	SOME ANIMAL STORIES	126
10	ALIENS, OR WHAT?	160
11	SOME MORE HEAD SCRATCHERS	181
12	THE LIFE BEYOND THIS LIFE	198
13	EPILOGUE	220
Index		224

... and other true stories

Acknowledgements

Where can I commence on such a mammoth task; remembering to thank everyone who in any way or many ways, helped to make this book a reality? Some of course are obvious, such as the sterling work of my long-suffering brother Bill whose work, setting up the book for digital printing, his help and advice and his overall patience, have ensured that the previous three books are so well finished.

We both, however, struggled with the cover. We had ideas, but neither of us is an artist.

Then at the very first meeting of our FAW (Fellowship of Australian Writers – Toronto NSW branch) for the year 2013 the president asked me where I was up to with the book. 'Fine,' I told her, 'except for the cover. That has me beat.'

Helen Marshall called out, I'll rattle up something for you, Lachlan.' Helen is a fine artist, and a writer. I thanked her but didn't really expect to hear from her – not immediately anyway. As I worked away on the computer that evening, an email message popped up, from Helen. 'Have a look at this,' it read. There was an attachment. When I opened it, I could hardly believe my eyes! The cover was much as you see it here today. It's brilliant, and when I sent it off to my brother, he thought so too. Thank you, Helen, for a superb cover that really reflects the spirit of the book. By the way, that picture under the light: it's a painting of the famous 14th century Urquhart Castle, on the shores of Loch Ness. My wife Janet and I have wandered its lonely corridors and climbed it battlements overlooking the dark waters of Loch Ness. Helen put it there but didn't know we'd been there.

Then there are the many, many folk who have been prepared to let me tell their stories. It's often a big ask, for sometimes it brings up memories of the past... sad memories, frightening memories. Some have told me their story, then begged me not to use it, and naturally whatever they've told me, stays with me. All I can say is thank you, from the bottom of my heart, to you all.

There are the committed writers in our FAW group, forever encouraging, ever ready to assist with advice, always willing to critique. Dirk Visman's advice and editing skills proved invaluable. Many thanks Dirk – a good job well done.

Janet, of course, has been my main encourager, for she, unfortunate lady, has to live with me – not that I've ever heard her complain. All the same, the old saying is true: 'No one is a saint to his/her family,' meaning of course they know what he/she is really like!

Quite apart from those who have direct connection to the book, there are so many others: family and friends, some of whom have been prepared to proof-read, and readers who have enjoyed the other Lachlan Ness books and have written to tell me, who have cheered me and encouraged me time and again. Thank you for being so supportive and helpful, and for being there whenever I've needed an encouraging word. To you all, and to those who in my thoughtlessness I have surely missed, I say a very big and heartfelt THANK YOU.

Lachlan Ness

... and other true stories

For

Andrew, Pat, Alison, Chris, Heather, Rolf, James, Stewart, Marilene

With Love

WARNING!

This book contains some Christian content. Exposure has been known to change lives

Listen, I tell you a mystery

St Paul

... and other true stories

Welcome to 'Puddleby on Sea'

Welcome! Come in! This is 'Puddleby on Sea,' our house on the shores of Lake Macquarie, NSW Australia, which Janet and I share with the only two of our children now living at home. The other five have two feet and jobs, while these two, Tonkie the Tonkinese cat and Jock the border collie have four feet, and are content to be kept in ease and comfort by us, their devoted servants. Tonkie is asleep in a chair closest to the fire (of course), but it's too warm for Jock, so he's selected a cooler place in the house. He barked when you knocked, but it was token.

Anyway, it's great to see you at last for our fireside chat. I've been trying to get you here for ages, and as we make our way down to the living room and a welcome hot cocoa or chocolate and some of Janet's cake, I'd like to explain that our chat this evening is not a scientific discussion. The story of the giant spider I'm going to tell you about later could possibly stir some response from arachnologists, entomologists, arachno-heads various, as well as other scientifically-minded people. From my poor knowledge however, science needs something apart from memories to assess the veracity of what it is examining.

The texts you will find scattered through the talk will help you reflect on the fact that the world we live in is far from being merely material. It's also spiritual, and it has a Creator; the One Whom we call God. I've never had a chat quite like this one, so I hope it goes OK. You must be a bit interested, for at least you're here. I hope you don't flounce off irritably half-way through the evening. Stay for the coffee and Janet's fine cake, if nothing else.

It's (nearly) all Greek to me!

Within the Christian faith, there are differing opinions concerning some topics, and the question of ghosts is among them. Funnily enough, when it comes to a question of whether ghosts are real or not, the answer for me lies in the pages of the New Testament; in the original language in which the New Testament was written..

Some Christians, when asked if they believe in ghosts, will say they don't believe in them because they're Christian. If you ask me the same question I'll tell you I do, because I'm a Christian. Confusing? It shouldn't be. The evidence is there in the pages of the Greek New Testament. Greek was the universal language of the day, as English is today. I recall reading somewhere that the Greeks used to say that anyone who didn't speak Greek spoke 'bar-bar' or nonsense, which is the origin of the word 'Barbarian.'

The first mention in the New Testament of the word interpreted as 'ghost' as we understand it, occurs during a great storm on the Sea of Galilee. The time is about 3.00am, and the disciples are out there in a boat, which is making heavy weather of it. Suddenly they see a figure approaching them across the waves, and they are terrified. 'It's a ghost!' (*phantasma*: 'ghost' or 'apparition' from where we get the English word 'phantom') they cry.

Jesus calls back 'Take courage! It is I. Don't be afraid.' (Matthew 14:22-33). He doesn't exclaim, 'Don't be silly – there are no such things as ghosts!'

Mark chapter 6:45-52 tells the same story, and the same Greek word for 'ghost' is used.

The next occasion occurs just after the resurrection, when a different word for 'ghost' is used by Luke, who was a Gentile - a Greek. (Non-Jews were known to the Jews as Gentiles. He is the only known, non-Jewish writer in the New Testament). The disciples were assembled, possibly in the upper room, when suddenly Jesus appeared among them. 'They were startled and frightened, thinking they saw a ghost.' (*Pneuma*: wind or spirit, or interpreted in this case, ghost).

Jesus reassured them: 'Look at my hands and my feet. It is I myself! Touch me and see; a ghost (*pneuma*) does not have flesh and bones, as you see I have." (Luke 24:37-39.

Pneuma or pneumatos is usually translated as 'wind' or 'spirit' but both the NIV (New International Version) of the Bible and Revised Standard Version (RSV), interpret it as 'ghost' because, I suspect, the body of the text suggests that translation.

As in English, there are many words in the Bible that have widely differing meanings and definitions, and cannot be translated too literally. Sometimes they have to be interpreted through their use in the sentence. (Here's an example in English: 'The team didn't stand a ghost of a chance' which obviously has nothing to do with the literal meaning of 'ghost').

It's quite obvious from those readings that Jesus believed in ghosts and makes that plain to the disciples.

The other word I want to run past you is the word 'ghoul.' You'll search the scriptures in vain for any reference to that word. My authority is the Concise Oxford Dictionary, which defines it as a superstition; a spirit preying on corpses, but again, that is the literal meaning. The word is from the Arabic word *gūl:* 'protean desert demon.' The word 'protean' means that it is able to assume many forms.

The latter is the meaning I would like to apply to the word 'Ghoul'; in other words, a demon; but just your average demon; nothing to do with one preying on corpses.

Generally, people in the former generations appear to have been able to accept the presence of the unseen world around us a lot more easily than many people in this generation. John Bunyan's beautiful 17th century hymn that commences *Who would true valour see* carries the lines:

Hobgoblin nor foul fiend
Can daunt his spirit.

Again, you'll search the scriptures in vain for any mention of hobgoblin or fiend, foul or otherwise, (although the Concise Oxford

Dictionary identifies 'fiend' as 'demon' or 'evil spirit' and there are plenty of those mentioned in the New Testament). At least we have in Bunyan's words, an acknowledgement of the other world, which, according to both Testaments of the Bible, as well as stories of countless numbers of people from every age and culture, exists. That knowledge seems to be wired into the human psyche.

Do you really believe it is all only make-believe?

My own earliest story: a supernatural incident

Let me start with a story that will set the tone for the evening. I'll remember the incident I'm going to tell you to my dying day. I was eight years old, standing beside my mother one evening as she chatted to a lady whose name I can still remember: Fay Bulgarie, although that is only my guess as to the correct spelling of her surname. I was, after all, only eight years old, but that's what it sounded like.

It was a lovely, warm evening in Leeton, NSW, heart of the Murrumbidgee Irrigation Area. I recall gazing up at the great, majestic, star-sprinkled universe, for there was nothing much else to see; certainly no bright lights to pale the beauty of the night sky, the way they do in the cities.

I can't recall thinking of anything in particular that night. I was certainly not interested in the conversation going on beside me, and I don't even think I was paying particular attention to the night sky. It was just there. When one lives out on the plains country, there's a lot of sky, with not a hill to obscure any of it. At night, well away from towns and cities, the sky, with its myriad stars and planets, all particularly bright on moonless nights, dominates all.

As with most children forced to stand beside adults who are engaged in adult conversation I was probably bored, waiting for my mother to go back into the house as I stared vacantly up at the stars.

What I saw electrified me. Suddenly, out of the heavens, among the stars, a hand and arm emerged. It was white, and I think (but can't swear to it), opaque. It appeared to be very large among the shining stars. The hand appeared to make a scooping motion. What I saw didn't simply vanish, but withdrew, the way it had appeared. Imagine a stage, with curtains that overlap a little. On the other side, someone slides an arm through the overlap, and you see it. (That is not a description of what I saw – it's the only way I can describe the way it appeared; seemingly from out of nowhere). You cannot see the actual opening when curtains overlap, which you would have, if they simply met. All you would see would be the arm and hand extended, seemingly without a body attached. The hand and arm I saw seemed to appear just like that, appearing from, then returning behind, the 'curtain,' as I've described it. I can only think of its appearing as from another dimension. I screamed to my mother to look, but of course by the time she looked, all she saw was the night sky.

She probably gave me a pat on the head and said, 'Yes, dear,' before continuing her conversation with Mrs Bulgarie.

I remember feeling nettled, frustrated that the magnitude of what I'd just seen was ignored. Mind you, I can hardly blame my mother for her reaction, which probably would have been the reaction of most parents. At least she didn't accuse me of making it all up, or chide me for interrupting her conversation with Mrs Bulgarie.

I had no sense at that time that what I had seen was a message directed to me particularly, like a message from God.

Now for a lighter side of that story: A couple of weeks ago I had a letter from my brother, Peter, who lives in Melbourne. I'd told him I intended to include the story I just related. I was surprised to learn that he remembers the incident very well, and reminded me of something that happened that night that I had conveniently forgotten. He said that when my mother and I were back in the house and I was excitedly telling my father about it, little Peter (aged six) decided that he wanted to get in on the action too. He ran outside, then ran back inside, exclaiming that he saw the same thing. Of course he hadn't, and I was very angry that my brother was trying to steal my thunder, and a fight followed. I can't remember the fight or even his running outside for a slice of the 'glory,' but he has the memory of an elephant for things that happened years ago. The upside is the fact that his letter confirms the truth of the incident; the downside is, I feel very sorry that I attacked my kid brother for doing what one would expect a little brother or sister to do; but then, I was only eight years old myself.

When I explained again to my mother the next day what I had seen, I am sure she believed me, but it was a moment that had gone and there is no way an eight year-old child could have described it; at least, not in any convincing detail.

The doubters of course will say that I was simply a bored child, and with bored children, anything is possible. I can see them now, smiling disbelievingly and nodding in that rather pitying way. 'Of course it didn't happen. You said you were bored, just looking at the stars. It's natural to have imagined it, and now you really believe it – may even have believed it then. Imagination can play tricks with our minds.'

I certainly did not make up the story I've related here. If I had been bored enough to make up a story, what I did see that night would never have entered my young head. I was into Spitfires and Hurricanes, warships and pirates, cowboys and Indians and other things that excited my boyish dreams at age eight, which was the year that saw the end of World War 2.

My hero back then was the singing cowboy, Gene Autry. He was frequently starring in the Saturday afternoon matinees at Leeton's one and only picture theatre, The Roxy.

There are few people to whom I've related that story; mostly only family members. I've discovered over the years that the usual response of someone who hears a story like that is to start looking around for a logical explanation... maybe it was a cloud, or smoke, or mist or… whatever one fancies, so long as it can be passed off with a logical explanation. The thing is, I've yet to see a cloud, mist, smoke or anything else that in any way resembles what I saw, which was a perfectly formed arm and hand, appearing from some other dimension (I suppose), then withdrawing back into it.

If you believe I saw what I actually did see – congratulations. Many will doubt it.

Janet and I spent three months of 2012 in central western NSW, where I did some supply ministry in the parish of Coolah-Dunedoo.

It is beautiful country out there, and like Leeton all those years ago, there is not a light strong enough out there to pale the blackness of the night sky, apart from a full moon.

On most nights while we were out there, I stood for a time out in the back garden, about 11.00pm, giving Jock our border collie his last run around the half-acre manse grounds, and a final chance to visit his 'loo for the night.

These days, I'm drawn increasingly to the beauty of the night sky. It is black out there before the moon decides to rise, and its beauty is breathtaking. The stars blaze down, like carelessly sprinkled handfuls of diamonds, with the Milky Way running through them like a winding, misty, magic roadway, seemingly going on for ever and ever.

I keep an eye out for the Southern Cross, which by then is on its journey across the sky.

Always I search with hope for another revelation like the one I saw one night so long ago. My eyes return to the spot in the sky where my memory tells me it took place.

In time, when I 'meet my Maker, face to face' I hope He, as Lord of all, explains it to me.

Ghosts

1

... and other true stories

The Ghost of old 'Fortuna'

As told by Major John Bloor (Ret'd)

I've known Major John for over twenty-five years. We met in Western Australia where John was the 2IC of his unit (2nd in command). Later he was made OC (Officer Commanding), and I was an Army chaplain posted to Western Australia. John and his wife Deirdre were both members of the Military Christian Fellowship (MCF) and it was from there that our friendship grew. Deirdre was a registered nurse, working in a Perth hospital. Spouses are included in the membership of the MCF.

John spent his military career in the Royal Australian Survey Corps.

When he was a young soldier he was posted to the Army Survey Regiment at 'Fortuna', in Bendigo, the great old mansion that had been built originally by George Lansell, the man who discovered gold there in the 19th century.

The gold brought George enormous wealth, and so he was in a position to indulge himself well in Fortuna's furnishings and gardens, which included a picturesque lake.

The house and gardens are most imposing. Take your carriage through the large, ornamental gates, clip-clop past the lake, where a little farther on the road rises, and you find yourself on a low plateau.

Soon after, you find yourself at the first of the two barrack blocks which housed the soldiers who were posted there.

John told me his quarters were in the first barracks block.

Give the reins a flick and your horse will obligingly trot on past the barracks blocks, to arrive eventually at the regimental kitchen door of Fortuna.

Looking from the barrack block, the kitchen building appears to be L-shaped. The road stops at the kitchen entrance which has an outer door, an airlock and an internal door which leads into the kitchen proper.

John was on an early morning shift, which commenced at 05.00 so was walking to work at about 04.45.

As he crossed the road, something caught his eye – something that he didn't expect to see, so he turned to see what it was.

What he saw transfixed him. The object that had caught his attention appeared at first to be 'something like a shroud,' as he described it, moving slowly from side to side outside the kitchen door.

Suddenly the young soldier realised what at first his senses had failed to accept. With a shock he found himself looking at a ghost.

The apparition continued to move outside the kitchen door as if looking for something. It was about 6 feet tall in the old scale but the face itself was not clear… more like a dark shadow.

It moved through the kitchen door and stood at the airlock for about half a minute, before moving back to where he first saw it, where it stopped abruptly. John had the impression that it was looking at him. It then turned away and moved to its right down near the windows, and as it moved, John noted that he could see the brickwork of the building through it. He shifted his position to get a better view. The apparition was now standing under a window before moving back to the kitchen door, where it vanished. John moved briskly to his place of work in the Air Survey Squadron building to start his shift.

About two hours later other members began arriving for the morning shift. One of them took in his appearance.

'You look very pale, John - in fact you look like you've seen a ghost!'

He meant it as a joke – until John said 'I have!' and went on to explain. (We have to use our imaginations here, and realise that John would not be speaking as you are reading the words on the printed page. In my mind I can see him looking pale and shaken and his voice pitch has gone up a notch or two… This man has just seen a real, 'live' ghost!)

The word went around and John found himself fronting the RSM (Regimental Sergeant Major), who was quite intrigued by the story.

'Fortuna' was well-known as a haunted house among soldiers who'd been posted there, and another soldier had reported seeing the same apparition that John had, on a different occasion, many years later.

Incidents happened in the old house that were inclined to make its earthly occupants a trifle on the nervous side. One evening, John recounted, the Duty Officer opened a door to make sure it was locked and discovered it was not. He opened the door and immediately heard a woman's voice demand: 'What are you doing here?' There had been no one in the room.

It turned out that the room in question was the bedroom of George Lansell's wife.

Quite a number of soldiers have told me stories of 'Fortuna' during their time there, many, many years before writing a book of this nature had ever occurred to me. They simply told me stories of their own ghostly encounters there, but John's tops the lot.

Major Bloor is a friend and a man of integrity, whose feet are firmly planted on the ground; an essentially practical, professional soldier who has never been given to practical jokes or flights of fancy.

There is no doubt in my mind: 'Fortuna' is haunted.

Subsequent to this story being given to me, I heard a radio news item that old 'Fortuna' passed out of the hands of federal government, into private ownership. It hadn't been used by the Defence Force for some time. The federal government had been attempting to continue ownership but apparently it wasn't possible to get the paperwork in at the appointed time, so now it is privately owned – ghosts and all, no doubt. The chequered history of the old mansion continues.

The Ghost in Croydon House, London

The following is part of a story sent in a letter to me by Wendy. She and her husband Tom are friends of ours and this incident occurred in London, while on holiday from Zimbabwe. At the time they were staying with their London friends, Mike and Linda

'We left Linda and Mike and continued on our holiday. On our return from Scotland we returned to their flat. Linda and Mike had gone off to the Isle of Man so we were alone there. Tom (my husband) had to return to London to get a copy of a birth certificate from Somerset House so said he would take the train after we had finished breakfast. I decided to do some washing, for we were returning to Zimbabwe the next day. I saw Tom off, then locked the front door before going upstairs to gather the clothes to be washed. It was very quiet in the flat as I busied myself, but suddenly I heard the front door open and close. I called out, thinking that Tom had forgotten something.

There was no reply, but as I headed for the top of the stairs I distinctly heard footsteps coming up towards me. I expected to see Tom – but there was no one there. Despite searching the house, I found no one else in it. I was the only one.

Strangely enough there was no sinister feeling in the room, so I can only suppose that if there was a ghostly presence, it bore me no ill-will.'

Wendy Randall

Somehow, the ghostly world around us seems to be able to interact with us, with sounds such as footsteps. Doors are known to open and close. Footsteps are common.

The Ghost in the Mausoleum

Quite a few years ago, my friend Stan told me an unusual story. He and his wife Betty were on holiday in North Queensland and were passing through the town of Ingham, which is surrounded by sugar cane farms.

With time on their hands, Stan and Betty decided to explore the town, which took them to the town cemetery, with its many mausoleums, most of which are owned by farmers of Italian background.

Walking along the empty streets of mausoleums was like walking along streets of houses in a town: small and large, ornate and plain – a true 'necropolis' – (Necros: dead. Polis: city. A city of the dead).

One mausoleum in particular caught their eye, for it was unusually ornate, and they stopped to admire it. In the middle was a door-sized panel of glass, enclosing a recessed area in which they could see various ornaments, such as a cross, artificial flowers and a photo or two, probably of the mausoleum's occupants. The mausoleum was so unusual that Betty decided to take a photo of it, which she did.

A couple of weeks passed. They enjoyed their holiday, went home and had the holiday photos developed (no digitals back then). When they looked at the photo of the mausoleum, they were astounded to see what appears to be the figure of a dark-headed woman behind the glass panel. She appears to be looking down to her left and is dressed in old-fashioned clothes. Immediately questions arise: Was it a reflection of Betty? (No way – not unless Betty changed her clothes and hairstyle and appeared older). Was someone in there? (Impossible. There's no door into that area – it's just a recess in the wall, and besides there was no one else at the cemetery at the time).

I was really curious and asked Stan if I could see the photo. Stan told me it was around somewhere but he hadn't seen it for a while. I was disappointed not to be able to examine it myself and more or less forgot about it - until I decided to tell these yarns. I wrote to Stan and Betty and asked if they would see if they could find the photo.

Not long after, they found it! I was quite excited, and have it here to show you. As you can see, it's quite an amazing photo, and the outline of the lady is quite plain to see. 'There was definitely no one near the place when I took that photo!' Betty told me emphatically. Make of it what you will… trick of the light? I can't see how that's possible. I think it's a genuine photo of a ghostly figure, but I leave it up to you to make up your mind.

The ghost that used 'Dencorub'

Now here is a rather odd story, told to me by Cheryl, whom I know. She's a very practical lady who holds a responsible management position. When an uncle died, she said, she inherited an old desk that she had often admired. When she got it home, she and her husband took it to pieces and reduced it to no more than a pile of timber. They then proceeded painstakingly to strip every single ounce of paint or varnish off every part, until it was all back to white wood. After that, they varnished it, before putting it back together again. Once again it was a handsome desk, and looked brand new.

A few weeks later, as she worked in the kitchen, one of her sons called out, 'Mum – have you been polishing your desk with 'Dencorub' or something?'

Puzzled, Cheryl went to investigate. When she walked into her office, the smell of Dencorub around the desk nearly bowled her over. She decided to ring her aunt to tell her the story.

'Cheryl,' her aunt replied, 'you remember your uncle - he suffered from lumbago and various joint and muscle aches and pains. He was forever rubbing Dencorub into his muscles. Whenever we smelt it when he was alive, we knew he wasn't far away.'

The Mischievous Ghost in the Manse

This is a strange little story. I myself have stayed in the manse (the name some churches use for the minister's dwelling) mentioned in this story, taking services during the holidays of the present incumbent. It's a very fine house anyone would be proud to live in. Sometimes it's hard to say if there is anything unusual about some incidents that occur in life, so it's best when they can be verified by others. The lady who tells the following story, and her husband, and the present minister, and I myself, have all had some unusual experiences in that manse, which does make one wonder... anyway, here is Joan's story:

Last year we took my brother and sister to the Blue Mountains, to catch the train to Sydney. The train was not due to leave until after lunch, so we decided to take our lunch and eat it in the Manse. The minister, a friend of ours, had given us a key to get in before he got back later in the day.

There is a kitchen sink and bench area between the dining room and kitchen, with a built-in dishwasher. We were seated at the table, eating our lunch, when we became aware of a rumbling noise in the kitchen. When we investigated, we found the dishwasher had started working, churning away merrily. My husband opened the dishwasher door, where we discovered that despite the water splashing about in the machine, there were no dishes in it. Neither of us had touched the dishwasher, and it had not been set to start working. In fact it is rarely used. No one had been in the house for a few days, until our arrival shortly before. An electrician was called in to have a look at the machine, who after examining it told us that it was not possible for it to have started without assistance.

Another story from the same manse:

It's a cold day in late winter in the year of grace, 2012.

A preacher sits quietly in a lounge chair in the manse, staring at the blank TV, contemplating just what he would say at the funeral service of a man whom he has never met; whose service he is to conduct in the church in less than an hour.

While sitting quietly, looking at nothing in particular, he becomes aware of something entering his peripheral vision. A figure, dressed in the garb of many years ago, moves across the room, having materialised from out of a blank wall. There is no sound of footsteps or anything else from the figure as it walks quickly across the room, through the walls and dining-room table and disappears.

What does our preacher say, during the service, of what he had just seen? Certainly nothing about his vaporous visitor.

I know the preacher. I know the manse. Nothing would surprise me about that manse!

The mysterious ghost at Kanwal

This story is definitely a poser. It was told to me by Ken, whom I've known for some years and he's hardly a man to make up stories. He holds a responsible administrative position in a government department that I visit regularly in my work as a part-time police chaplain. He's a no-nonsense, down to earth type whose working world is figures, statistics and other mysteries beyond my ken, as it were. He told me the story over morning tea one day; an incident that was shared by three others.

'It happened a few years ago,' said Ken. 'My wife Cheryl and I and two friends were in a car, returning from a function. It was rather late at night, and we were on our way home on the Central Coast. On our left was Cragie Park, and beyond that, the lake. We were making a turn off Donald Avenue, into Edna Avenue. On the right was a vacant block, although there's a house there now.

I glanced out to the right – and nearly lost control of the car! I saw what appeared to be a glowing orb of light, moving slowly through the high grass in the vacant block, causing it to part, just as if a person were walking through it. It shook me, but I just kept driving. There was complete silence in the car.

About a kilometre on, I asked rather shakily, 'Did anyone see what I saw back there?'

The three replies were as one: 'Yes!' Everyone had seen it – but just what we all saw – that's the question.

'I'll never forget it,' said Cheryl, with a bit of a shudder. 'He was a ghost – an old man. I could see he was wearing a chequered shirt – but I could see through it. He was sort of semi-transparent, and sort of glowed. He seemed to be floating, but the grass was parting as he floated through it.'

'Yes – yes, that's exactly what I saw!' exclaimed our friend's wife, from the back seat. 'It was frightening!'

'No, no – it was nothing like that!' interrupted her husband; 'It was like a ball, or orb of light. There wasn't any person there!'

'And that is the strangest thing,' Ken told me. 'We men saw only an orb of light, with the grass parting before it as it moved. Both women saw a ghost in a chequered shirt. Explain that, if you can!'

I wouldn't even attempt to try, but later I spoke to Cheryl, who verified Ken's account, and later she sent me a Google map, with the position of the sighting marked on it.

The girl in the chequered shirt

You will note that many of these stories are of ghosts who don't seem to have any connection whatsoever with the earthly folk they confront. They are simply 'there.'

I remember a story told to me by a fellow I know very well, whose name is Bill Oakey.

He told me once that when he was about twenty years of age, he stayed overnight at a friend's unit at Maroubra (a Sydney suburb), rather than try to find his way home late at night, for they'd been to a party.

Some time in the 'wee sma' hours' (Scottish: late at night, early morning), he said, he awoke to see a girl with blonde hair sitting at the end of his bed.

I passed him a sceptical look. 'You were about twenty years of age? Are you sure her presence wasn't the combined effect of a night out and twenty million hormones raging through your young body?'

He grinned. 'Could have been – but I don't think so. She wasn't my type. I mean, I could see that she was wearing a chequered shirt – but I could also see the wall on the other side through her, so I knew she wasn't of this world. I wasn't frightened. In fact she had a peaceful sort of presence. I told my friend the next day and of course he laughed. He didn't believe it. There is, however, a really odd ending to this story,' continued Bill. 'My friend was quite stunned when some time later his flatmate, who'd never met me and hadn't been told my story, said he'd seen a ghost, and described in exact detail what I'd seen.'

My encounter in the caravan

By LS

'I was in my twenties. My parents were in their caravan at the time on a long holiday, working their way around Australia, but at that point they were at a caravan park not far from where I was working as a nurse. Usually, I lived in the nurses' quarters, but with my parents so close by for a time, I stayed with them on my days off, before they left again on their travels.

Attached to their caravan was an annex, which I used as my sleeping quarters. The flaps at the entrance were always open, but the park was quiet, and I soon got used to it.

One night, however, I was awoken by a mysterious ssshhhhhhh! sound. I hoisted myself up to see what was going on.

To my utter amazement, I saw the ghostly form of a man, who appeared to be a hooded monk. It landed softly on its feet like a bird; then walked right up to the very head of my bed and bent right over me, to look into my face.

In sheer terror I covered up my head with the blanket, and shrieked out, 'Muuuuumm!'

My mother was at my side in an instant. Knowing she was there, I uncovered my head and shakily told her about my strange supernatural experience.

'Darling!' Mum said in her usual soothing tone, 'I think that was your guardian angel!'

Hearing those comforting words, I was no longer afraid. I actually wanted my angel to come back. Each night I waited, but in vain. I guess he was making doubly sure that I was in a very deep sleep before he returned to watch over me.' (*Are not all angels ministering spirits sent to serve those who will inherit salvation? Hebrews 1:14*).

The ghost at the dressing table mirror

The following story was told to me by Joan, whom Janet and I know very well. We have stayed with her and her husband. They are the finest of people; practising Christians, mature in their faith and involved in the life of the Church. I doubt very much if either would be capable of telling even a small porkie, let alone a major one. Here is Joan's story:

A long time ago, I had a very elderly great uncle and aunt, (my father's uncle and aunt) living in Orange, who used to visit us from time to time, while at other times we went to stay with them. In time, my great aunt died, but we still visited my great uncle to keep an eye on him, and one of those occasions was shortly after my great aunt's death.

In my mind I can still picture it, although I was quite young at the time. My great uncle's and aunt's house was old-fashioned but comfortable, with a hallway running from the front door, and bedrooms off either side. My parents were in the main guest room which was the first room to the left, while my sister and I occupied one of the other bedrooms.

During the night, both my parents awoke to see the ghostly figure of my Aunt come through the closed front window of their room, sit in front of the dressing table, and brush her long grey hair. They felt no sense of fear. She hadn't been a fearful person in life and she wasn't in death – if you can call a ghost 'dead.'

Something woke me about the same time, and I became aware of a light, moving around in the hallway. I could see the glow, because my mother kept our bedroom door open, so that she could hear us if we called out to her in the night. I quietly woke my sister, and we watched wordlessly as the light came through our door and moved to the upper corner near the door before it faded away. During the whole visit of my Great Aunt's visit to her old house, not one of us made a sound – we were probably too overcome by amazement. I think there must have been some unnatural silence because during the visitation, my parents were acutely aware of my Great Uncle's snoring in his room.

A ghost story from Canada

Here is a story from someone we know in Canada, who told me the following story in person, a long time before I had contemplated putting all the stories together. I remembered he'd told me, for it's a strange one, so I rang him the other day to get his permission to pass it on to you, which he gave. Here it is:

'It had rained heavily all week, and on the night in question there had been a very heavy downpour; in fact so heavy that the rain found every spot in the roof where it could possibly leak through – and it did.

During the night I decided to get up and go downstairs to the basement, to check on how much rain was leaking into a bucket I'd placed there, in case it started to overflow.

As I got towards the bottom of the stairs, just in front of me I saw three ghostly figures of native American men, doing some sort of tribal dance which for some reason I assumed was a rain dance, given the circumstances. If that was so, they were certainly doing a good job. I still reflect on that incident, trying to analyse my feelings at the time, which I've come to think of as inexpressible. Maybe that's no surprise, when I think back on it. I went back upstairs without emptying the bucket and got back into bed, trying to make sense of what I had seen. It wasn't until some time later that I learned that the area on which our unit, and the other units in the block, had been built on a Native American burial site.'

The ghost nurse of old 'Southall'

Charles Moore (1820-1895) migrated to Australia from the UK and became a prominent citizen in Sydney, at one time serving as its Lord Mayor. He had the interests of the colony at heart and was responsible for developing the thousand acres known as 'Sydney Common' into a lovely park. During his lifetime, the Council renamed it 'Moore Park' by which that beautiful park in the heart of Sydney is known to this day.

Somewhere around the year 1880 he moved to the mansion he'd built in Springwood, in the Blue Mountains, next door to the Anglican Church, for he was a devout Anglican.

After his death, his lovely Springwood home passed through various hands. At one time it became 'Karkoola Maternity Hospital' for about twenty years, but some time after that it was bought as a private home by a retired hospital matron, Sister Sophie Durham, who named the house 'Southall' after the town in England where she was born.

Matron Durham died in the hallway of 'Southall' and the home was sold to the grandparents of a friend of mine, who told me a strange story that had been told him by his mother, who'd been told it by her parents.

Not only did I have the opportunity to speak to Moya, my friend's mother who lived in 'Southall', she invited me to speak to her mother, Mrs Hibbard, now in her nineties but still with a sharp and active mind. Her husband was a builder, and he set about restoring 'Southall' to its former glory, which over time he achieved.

It was a delight to speak to both those gracious ladies and I only wish I had time to retell some of the marvellous stories of old 'Southall' during the many years it was in the family, but it's not possible.

Mr Hibbard has passed on, but Mrs Hibbard remembers the incident well, for it involved her husband. It seems they had an evening routine: Mr Hibbard usually retired first and was followed some time later by his wife. One night, probably in the year 1968, and probably around 11 pm, Mrs Hibbard retired. Her husband, who was still awake, said,

'I've just seen a ghost!' Mrs Hibbard was alarmed at the news, but he replied that the apparition, in a nurse's uniform, had a caring and friendly face. 'She was smiling, and plumpish,' Colin Hibbard told his wife, 'and at a guess, about 40 to 45 years of age.' She was leaning over the bed, looking at him, he said, and as he looked up at her, she vanished.

The next morning, Mr Hibbard drew from memory a sketch of what he'd seen: a woman in a nurse's uniform, made distinctive by two scolloped edges on each collar, and a nurse's badge in the centre of the uniform at the throat. The badge was unusual in that its shape was long, rather than round or oval, and it was in a vertical position. Later, he showed the sketch he'd drawn to a family friend, a Mrs Pat Stanborough, who was a nursing sister, as her late mother had been before her. 'That's the uniform the nursing sisters wore in my mother's day!' she exclaimed.

'Having a ghost in the house gave me the creeps', Mrs Hibbard told me with a laugh, 'but I never saw it.'

One evening young Moya, her sister Noni and two friends were playing cards whilst babysitting their younger sister, Jayne, who was sleeping soundly, when they became thoroughly petrified because they heard footsteps in the hall when there shouldn't have been footsteps, for no one was there to make them. They heard it three separate times during the evening before their parents came home.

Mr Hibbard said on several occasions that he was sure he'd locked a door that was later found to be unlocked.

'Southall' eventually passed out of the family's hands and to the best of my knowledge is now an elegant and comfortable B&B that still carries the name 'Southall.' Should you wish to stay there you can choose one of three separate suites: the Vicarage Suite, the Karkoola Suite or the Durham Suite, each of which reflects the home's former days.

Whether or not a certain friendly nursing sister with a smiling face still walks what were once her wards, I've not heard.

A Ghostly Warning

By JM

The following story is from Jan, a friend of ours. I have known her and her husband for some time now through our writing group. She's a published author with two books and numerous articles to her credit over quite a few years, mainly to do with sailing, travel and the sea. She's originally from NZ but now lives in Australia. She spent her working life as a high school English teacher. Writing and speaking good English are subjects she's quite passionate about, so she's a marvellous person for new writers who need assistance with grammar, writing and anything to do with the English language.

Here is her story in a letter she sent me the other day…

'Around Christmas-time on a visit to Sydney, I was faced with my first supernatural experience. It was during my initial trip 'overseas' – across the Tasman from New Zealand.

Having completed my bachelor's degree, I flew from Christchurch to Sydney for a summer job. The work was organised by the University Students' Union. Along with other students from New Zealand and Australia, I was trained to sell 'Students' World Books' door to door. The organisers had arranged accommodation for us in various hostels, especially when we travelled out of Sydney

There is nothing like shared accommodation to promote camaraderie. We quickly developed friendships and my particular friend was a good-natured girl called Bev. She wore a cross around her neck and made no secret of her Christian beliefs. She was a devout Anglican. When Christmas approached, she asked me if I would like to share Christmas with her family. One of our group was a very outgoing young man named Rick, who was from Reading in England. As he was so far from home, Bev extended her invitation to Rick as well. I had made no plans for Christmas, so was thrilled to be invited to share Christmas with Bev, her brother Gary and their mother.

Rick, Bev and I travelled to her home in Western Sydney two days before Christmas Eve. The small three bedroom house had twin beds in Bev's and her brother's rooms. Rick shared with Gary and I shared with Bev. Rick seemed to take all that was offered to him as a matter of his right. I had liked him when I first met him, but seeing him at Bev's place, I began to notice his arrogance.

Without asking permission, Rick picked up Gary's guitar and began strumming it. He didn't offer to help with chores or seem to realise the sacrifices Bev's mother made for her kids. She was a war widow and life on her pension wasn't easy. Despite her tight financial circumstances, Bev's mother made both of us very welcome and even bought Christmas gifts for us. Like Bev, she was a true Christian, happy to open her home to others.

When we had finished watching television one evening between Christmas and New Year, Gary declared he wasn't tired yet and wasn't ready to go to bed. The rest of us agreed we would rather stay up a while too.

We remained seated where we had been after Mrs Brown had retired to bed. We played a game of cards.

'What will we do now?' asked Gary when the game was finished.

'Why don't we have a séance?' suggested Bev.

I was about to agree when I sensed another person had entered the room.

'No, no we can't,' I muttered.

I watched the shadowy figure move around the room and became aware the others could see it too. Their eyes were following the figure. It had to be a ghost. Its feet seemed to glide just above the floor. It had emerged through the closed door of the laundry. The time was close to midnight. The sitting room was silent. The figure swanned across to Rick and stopped behind his chair. The ghost was a tall, well-built older man in a dark suit. He placed his hands on Rick's shoulders. Rick seemed to shrink. He slunk down in his chair as though those hands were pushing him down. There was a sense of warning in the air.

After a few moments, the ghost lifted his hands and glided away. He exited the room through the wall to the outside.

When I looked at Rick again, he was still hunkered down in his chair, his face pale.

'Did – you – lot - see - what I saw?' I asked in a small voice.

Bev said, 'Yes, I saw it.'

'Me too,' said Gary.

Rick just nodded. Some of his bravura seemed to be returning now the threat had disappeared. Colour was returning to his face.

'I think it is time we went to bed,' said Bev.

The rest of us agreed. We prepared for bed and Bev and I were soon sound asleep. I awoke before the rest of the household next morning. I dressed quietly and went into the living room, where I wandered around looking at photographs on display. On the mantelpiece, there was a photograph of the man who had been our ghost the previous evening.

When Bev came through, I pointed to the photo. 'Who's this?'

'Oh, that's Grandpa,' she said, giving me a strange look.

'Where does he live?'

'He used to live with us, but he died about four years ago.'

'He was the ghost last night?'

'Yes. He looks after me.'

'You've seen him before?' I asked.

Bev nodded. 'Oh yes. Quite often.' I looked at Bev's hand, which was clutching her gold cross. 'He gave me this,' she said, looking at the pendant I was staring at.

We said nothing more about the incident at that time. Student's World required us back at work early in the New Year. They provided transport to take us to Canberra.

When our jobs were over. Bev went home and I completed my Sydney holiday. Before I flew home, I went out to Lidcombe to visit Bev and her mother.

'Did you ever see Rick again after we finished work?' Bev asked me.

'No, he just left without telling anyone.'

'He came back here,' Bev told me quietly

'Had you invited him?'

'No. After that incident, I didn't trust him anymore,' said Bev, with a little shudder

'What did he say when he turned up?'

'We didn't actually see him, but I knew it had to be him.'

I stared at her. 'Why? What happened?'

'He climbed in through Gary's bedroom window and stole Gary's guitar and a few other things – some money and clothes. Do you remember how much he liked my brother's guitar?'

'Yes, I did notice how he liked to play it without asking. But are you sure it was Rick?'

Bev nodded. 'We went to the police. Rick James wasn't his proper name. They found that out from the immigration records. No Rick James entered the country. There was no record of him at all. It seems that much of what he told us about himself were just lies.'

'So that's what your grandfather was warning you about!'

'That's what I believe.'

I have never forgotten that night. Whenever someone declares ghosts to be non-existent, I remember the warning Bev's Grandfather gave us about Rick or James or whatever was his real name.'

What is particularly interesting about this story is the number of people who saw the apparition at the same time, which is unusual. Many who believe that supernatural experiences are the result of over-fertile imaginations have often pointed out that few can produce a witness or witnesses. Just one story that can be verified by others helps give credibility to the supernatural world that exists. I have a suspicion that many who claim that there is nothing outside the five senses, are governed by fear of the unknown.

The Swaggie Ghost of Gravesend

June is a lady whom I've known for some time. One day a couple of years ago, I dropped in to her house on a pastoral visit, for she was a member of the congregation where I was filling in at the time. As we chatted over a cuppa and sticky bun, the conversation got around to various topics of interest, mainly to do with church and other matters.

June suddenly asked 'Did I ever tell you about the time my husband and I saw a ghost?' I told her she hadn't.

'We were away from home at the time, up around the town of Gravesend, in North-West NSW. Do you know the area?'

'Not well, but we have friends who have a property up that way.'

'Right. Well, my husband and I were driving along a bush dirt road, if you could call it that, up that way, well off the beaten track. There was nothing out there, except the bush. Suddenly, my husband jammed on the brakes. I looked up to see why he'd stopped so suddenly – and then I saw why.

Approaching us, off the road to the left, was a swaggie, as large as life, with his old bushman's hat on his head and his swag under his arm, with his tin billy hanging from it. We just stared in amazement. There aren't many swaggies left these days, as you know. They don't 'hump their blueys' these days, the way they used to, back in Henry Lawson's time, so you can imagine our surprise – but a bigger surprise awaited us. If he kept walking on his present course, we could see that he would walk into the bonnet of our car – which is exactly what he did. Our hair stood on end as he walked *through* the bonnet, across to the other side of the road where he seemed to follow some long-gone track. We watched him until he disappeared into the bush. It wasn't until he'd disappeared that it really dawned on us that we'd been watching a ghost.'

I stared at June, open-mouthed. 'That's an amazing story, June!'

'And it's true – every word of it.'

I never doubted her, even for a second. June is not the person to make up a strange story like that, for she's as honest as the day. Here is another of those inexplicable incidents when an apparition – this time of a swagman, was seen by two quite sane people during an afternoon drive. I hope this story gives those who may be sceptical, a time to pause and ponder and wonder.

Ghostly hands – for good and for evil.

What do I mean, when I talk about 'invisible hands'? Well, I do confess it's a bit of a mystery. Jesus, when assuring the disciples it was He, said, *Touch me and see; a ghost (pneuma) does not have flesh and bones, as you see I have.* (Luke 24:37-39).

Over the years I have been told by a number of people of 'hands' that touched them or grabbed them, or moved items in the house and did other things that ordinary 'ghostly' type beings are not capable of doing. Perhaps these come under the category of 'poltergeist' activity. Not all ghostly hands seem bent on mischief.

I know I am repeating myself when I ask you not to ask me to explain, for I can't because I don't know the answer. I am simply telling you the stories as they were told to me, by people who, I know, are not lying.

Here is an example told me by a lady whom I will call Heather.

She told me that when she was a little girl aged about five or six, she found herself locked in a room of the family home with her little brother. She can't remember how the door came to close, but it was reasonably dark in there and she was terrified. The fact that her little brother was screaming did not help.

For some reason, she couldn't work up the courage to reach the door so stood there, frozen with fear. Suddenly, she felt herself 'propelled' towards the door as an invisible hand pushed her. It was so strange, she told me, and there was no mistaking the hand at her back.

Once she was there, she could open the door. 'There was no one there in the room with us,' she said, 'and it was certainly not my little brother, who at the time was only a baby.'

Most of the stories however are not helpful hands, as they were in that particular case. I'd like to see this incident in the light of a guardian angel.

The Hair-Pulling Ghost in Croydon Park, old London Town

You may recall an earlier story that was told to me by Wendy. She wrote to tell me the story of the strange ghost in Croydon House, London. Well, here's another story from her. This story is a continuation of the time she and her husband Tom were sharing a flat in Croydon Park, London, with friends

Wendy and her husband are devout, practising Christians. Here is the story in her words:

'The year was 1978 and my husband Tom and I were on holiday in England. We were staying with friends Linda and Chris at their flat in Croydon which was a typical upstairs/downstairs apartment. Tom and Linda and I were in the kitchen preparing dinner when suddenly I felt a strong tug on my hair. Neither Linda nor Tom was near me and they both denied touching my hair. It was a real pull on my hair and of course I turned at once, expecting to see Chris, but there was no one. In any case, it would have been an extraordinary thing for Chris to do, completely out of character.'

I have been told on numerous occasions of similar stories of hair-pulling spooks, or poltergeists. Those beings, whatever they are, appear to be bent on mischief rather than malevolence. I must point out that I don't go around asking people about those things. People tell me and I am interested, and note them down in my diaries.

There is another account of mysterious hands in another chapter in the book, connected to Tarot cards. See the chapter 'The Question of Evil.'

Hauntings

2

'Lang Syne' - The Haunted Farm House

It's cosy and pleasant here at 'Puddleby,' sipping hot chocolate, and right now that other, mysterious world seems so far away. I would, however, like to tell you a story concerning *Lang Syne*, our old farm in Leeton. That it was haunted, I have no doubt whatsoever; nor has any member of our family who has lived there.

My grandfather acquired the farm in the first quarter of the twentieth century as a 'deceased estate.' Grandfather (known to us a Papa), was a successful farmer and in time he and his two sons (my father and his brother) turned the farm into a magnificent citrus orchard. 'Pioneer' tourist buses used to call there. Old Papa made his mark in the town and was on the founding board of Directors that established "Letona' cannery in Leeton (now sadly defunct). He was wealthy enough to purchase a new Dodge car every year, but in other ways – especially with his family, he was quite mean. My father said that he kept the pantry locked. If my grandmother wanted something, she had to ask him for the key. As well, he liked to say grace before meals which went along the lines: 'For what we are about to receive, Lord, make us truly thankful, and go easy on the butter, it's 2/6 a pound.' (Two shillings and sixpence – about 30 cents). Half the grace was for the Lord's ears, and half for the family's ears, my father said!

Prior to my grandfather's purchase of the property, *Lang Syne* had a sad history.

According to the story conveyed to us, the first owner, Charles McAlister, hanged himself in one of the farm sheds. His wife (so the story goes, as told by my father, who learned it from his father), developed a mental illness ('went mad' to use my father's graphic description) and finally died. Her husband had a beautiful black horse, which he rode around the farm. No one else was allowed to ride it. One day a farm hand took the horse for a ride. The horse fell and broke its leg and had to be put down. It was that incident, it seems, that was the final straw, and the sad man took his own life.

My cousins, (my father's brother's children) were also told this story.

The farm's sad history continued after it passed into our family. One day in 1942, my grandfather climbed up onto a shed roof, unaware that the termites had been there before him. The section he was standing on collapsed, and he fell through, broke his back and died.

My grandmother swore the following is true, but as she was given to flights of fancy, I can't guarantee it. She said that one evening, a couple of days before my grandfather's fatal plunge, a photo of him on the mantelpiece inexplicably toppled forward and fell. When they picked it up they were amazed to note that while the glass remained intact, the wooden back behind the actual picture had broken across.

That, my grandmother always said, was a portent.

After his unexpected death my grandmother went through all the accounts and discovered that large amounts of money could not be accounted for –they'd gone missing. Stories abounded of bank accounts under false names and even of money hidden around the old farm. My grandmother's efforts to track the missing money were in vain, so she decided to contact her husband 'on the other side.' She found a medium with a good reputation for being able to contact the dead and they held a séance in a room at *Lang Syne*. All the paraphernalia was in place – the candles, the dimmed lights, a photo of the deceased and so on. Finally the medium said 'I am in contact with your husband, Bob... yes... Bob is here in the room... ask him your question...'

My grandmother's question was terse and to the point: 'What did you do with the money, Bob?'

If old Bob was there, he refused to answer, and to this day its whereabouts remains a mystery. I still have a bit of a chuckle when I recall that story.

There was something very strange about *Lang Syne*. It never brought happiness. After their father's death, my father and his brother were forever at odds, constantly warring with each other.

That the house was haunted, not one of us who lived there has any doubt. Whatever it was, it was malevolent. My brother and I used to sleep with our blankets over our heads, aware of some presence in the room that exuded evil. We were terrified for no apparent reason, apart from what we could sense. 'It' (whatever it was) preferred to make its presence felt when only one person was in the house. I recall being there on various occasions, in the lounge room, absorbed in a book, when suddenly I'd know 'it' was there. Against my will, I would be drawn from my book as the hairs on the back of my head figuratively stood on end. None of us ever saw it; we felt an overriding sense of nameless terror, aware something evil, and not of this world, was watching us. It's impossible to explain it to someone who hasn't felt it. I would run out of the house and if it was winter, stand outside shivering for about fifteen minutes. When I went back in, driven in by the cold, all would be normal again. Similar experiences were shared by us all.

One night my father took us somewhere, leaving our mother at home alone. When we returned we found her outside, terrified and shivering. She told us the story: she was absorbed in her book in the lounge room when the terrifying feeling we'd all felt drew her out of it. Suddenly, she said, the lounge room door crashed open, accompanied by a roaring sound, and the sound of running footsteps down the hall.

Terrified, she ran outside, where we found her. When we went inside, 'it' had gone. All was normal once more.

There was a cellar just outside the back door where in the pre-refrigerator days, food such as butter was stored. My father thought 'it' lived down there. It never occurred to me to think where it lived.

In time, we moved off the farm, and my uncle and aunt and their children moved in. They had similar stories: *Lang Syne* was haunted.

Rice became a big earner for farmers around the district. Someone planted a rice crop not far from *Lang Syne* which raised the water table and drowned that beautiful orchard. The farm was eventually sold.

Many years later, I went back to the farm and spoke to the owners. The old house, which used to look so grand to us, with its wide verandahs and a certain air of elegance, looked old and small and tawdry. The verandahs had been walled in. The then owners told me they had not felt any unusual presence, evil or otherwise, so it seems 'it' has departed. Maybe it was something to do with our family.

My mother, although a Scot, wasn't 'fey' as many Scots are. As far as I know, she never had another paranormal encounter after we left *Lang Syne*. I'm sure she didn't want any more!

The old farm has well and truly passed out of our lives, and all the old people, and some of the younger ones, are now dead.

Other people bought the farm and it was cut up into five-acre blocks, with nice houses on them – but the old farmhouse is still there, guarding its own sad, dark secrets, brooding over its own tragic past. Who knows? Maybe it is still guarding the lost money.

Maybe, however, somewhere, my grandmother has met up with my grandfather again. If so, I wonder if she ever did get an answer to that question: 'What did you do with the money, Bob?'

Haunted Railway Stations

Have you heard of 'The Railway Children'? It's a delightful children's book, written by Edith Nesbit. Well, how about The Railway Ghosts? You may not be aware of it, but many who work for State Rail (NSW) believe St James station on the Sydney city circuit, is haunted. Staff members often hear voices from nowhere which are not speaking to the frightened listeners, but among themselves… chatter, laughter and so on, but there is no one anywhere near, and no other place from where voices of people (live people that is) could be emanating.

As I keep reminding you, I am not recording the words of people whose sanity may be suspect, but staff members I have spoken to, and know personally.

Another spot believed by many railway staff members to be haunted is the west wing of Central Station. I have been told (but have not verified) that the section of Central Station, somewhere near the country trains platform, was a morgue, many years ago.

For reasons of security and confidentiality I have to be careful not to reveal too much about those who have told me these things, long before there was any thought in my mind of passing on the stories.

One young woman told me of the fear she and others experience from time to time to this day when working late at night in their section. She told me that there is a long corridor on the way to the women's toilet, which requires a security card to enter the toilet area.

One night she went to the toilet and as she arrived at the door, ready to insert the card, she heard female voices in the locker room, laughing and chatting away. She had just left the only other people (about half a dozen or so) working away at their jobs and the rest of the building was locked down. There was no one who could possibly be in there, but she looked. It was empty. She fled.

All the others who work in that section have had similar experiences. Now, no one will visit there alone. At least two go together.

The Haunted Railway Tunnel

'I was approaching Central Station (Sydney) down such and such tunnel, doing approximately 70kph,' Sven told me a year or two back. It was not something about which I had approached him; he was telling me something of his life as a train driver, and this story had occurred only a couple of days previously. He was keen to share it, and I was keen to hear it.

'It's vun of der older tunnels,' continued Sven, who looks a bit like a Viking, 'and I've driven down it many a time. I had the signals and knew all ahead was clear. Suddenly, I was astonished to see up there in the darkness of the tunnel ahead, a red lantern, waving me to stop!

I could see that it was one of the types used a hundred years or more ago. I said to myself, 'How can this be? There is no way there can be anything ahead' but still the lantern was waving at me. What do I do? Well, I decided to ignore it. If there had been a problem I would have had word from the radio. I watched the waving lantern as the train got closer and closer, knowing that it was not possible for anyone to be there. Sure enough as the train drew level with the lantern, it vanished, and there was nothing there.'

I vos – I mean, was (sometimes Sven's accent gets to me) completely fascinated by my Swedish friend's amazing story. I've known him for years; a fine man who is treasurer of his church and certainly would not be prepared to tell a porkie like that – or any sort of porkie for that matter. I remember his telling me a year or two before, that staff members had told him of noises, like picks and shovels being worked, and voices, down some of those old railway tunnels around Central that have been abandoned for years.

I have no answer for those sorts of intriguing stories, except to say I know Sven, and some others who work for NSW Rail. I don't know of anyone who would want to make up yarns like that. I do know, however, that many would like to know the answers to those mysteries.

I'll leave you to work out the answer you favour, but in view of what I've been told, it seems to me that ghostly experiences down around certain areas of Central Station are real. All we can do is assign them to that area of the unseen world around us of which the Bible speaks. (Colossians 1:13-16 and numerous other texts).

The Haunted Castle

During my days as a chaplain in the Australian Regular Army (1976-1992), chaplains from the three services were given a week each year to go on 'retreat.' Well, I don't know about the Navy and the Air Force, but in the Army, 'retreat' is not a popular word, so we army chaplains went off on 'tactical withdrawals.'

We went according to denomination: Anglican, RC and PD. As a Presbyterian of course I was a PD ('Protestant Denominations', otherwise known as the 'odds and sods').

The PD chaplains from the three services went off together to a variety of places each year, and some were a bit on the rough side, but in my final three or four years in the Australian Regular Army, our Retreat was held at a Roman Catholic retreat house in Sydney, near the suburb of Double Bay, right on Sydney Harbour. It was a beautiful place, and the nuns who ran it were gracious and kind as well as remarkably efficient. We hardly ever saw them, and yet everything was there for us, and everything was immaculately clean and tidy. Each chaplain had a small, separate room with a desk, chair and bed, and of course a wardrobe for our clothes. Attire was civilian.

For much of the year we chaplains rarely saw one another, for we were at our postings at military establishments, Navy, Army, Air Force, around the country.

Those annual retreats of one week were stellar occasions for most of us, and it was on the retreats that we really got to know one another. Over the years most of us became good friends. Apart from the study, the services, and so on connected to the retreat activities, there were other, 'fun times' we used to organise among ourselves during our leisure times. Even now, thinking back on those days, *a host of kind faces is gazing on me* (words from the lovely old Welsh folk song, *The Ashgrove*. Those words by John Oxenford). Some of course have been gathered from 'the church militant to the church triumphant' (to frame it more vulgarly, they're dead), but the rest of us are still managing to dodge the undertaker.

One evening, some of us decided to have a 'story telling' session. Most of the stories were interesting, but not to the point of my being able to remember them all those years ago.

I still remember however, the story told to us by chaplain Gordon ('Haggis') Watson. He was a Scot, and a minister of the Uniting Church of Australia, and had come to Australia as an adult. I hope Gordon will forgive me for calling him 'Haggis' in this yarn. I'd ask him for permission but it was a long time ago and I don't know where he is now, but all the same, I use it with the same affection I had for him then.

I can't remember just what town it was where Haggis grew up, but on its edge was an old, ruined castle. Haggis was in the town pipe band and their place to practise was the one remaining, solid room in the castle. To get to the room was a bit of a challenge because it was not ground floor. The pipers had to climb narrow stone steps, up quite a long way. On one side was a wall, but on the other side there was nothing but space, so of course the higher one climbed, the greater became the danger of a fall with almost certain fatal consequences. One did not hurry up or down those stairs – particularly at night. Those were certainly pre-OH&S days!

Somehow the pipers had managed to get electricity connected to the room, for the band met in the evenings.

On the particular evening of which Haggis spoke, for some reason he stayed behind – probably to practise a little longer. When he went to leave he turned off the light and went to the door– and found himself in pitch darkness – no light of moon or star shone that night. Cautiously he began to edge his way down those terrible stairs. Half way down, he stopped for a moment – and then he heard it. I only wish I could describe better the way he told the story. He was a great story-teller and we were spellbound. 'Behind me, I heard footsteps! I knew I had been the last to leave that smallish room. They were shuffling footsteps... one slow step at a time, coming behind me. I tell you, my hair stood on end! It was terrifying. What was the ghostly presence following me down those stairs? At considerable risk tae life and limb, I hurried down a few more steps. Surely I must have been mistaken! I stopped – and there it was again.. that dreadful, slow, relentless shuffle – stop - shuffle –stop - shuffle... was following me down the stairs. I can't describe the nameless sense of dread I felt. I took a few more paces and stopped and listened. Yes – it was still following me, whatever it was.

Finally, I was down. There was a long sort of corridor leading out to the castle door, and along its length there were shallow alcoves. Even although I was terrified, I was also curious, so I ducked into one of the alcoves and waited. The slow, shuffling footsteps came closer and closer in the blackness until finally I could hear them passing me. I stood there breathlessly, listening, expecting them to disappear into silence out the door. I was amazed when instead of that, the footsteps made a sound that I associated with going down yet more steps, until I could hear them no more. As far as I knew, there was nothing beyond the front door, which was to one side of the corridor or hallway. As soon as I could, I bolted out of the castle and fled.

In the calm light of the next day, recalling the incident and the sound of the steps disappearing down more stairs, I decided to investigate.

When I did, I discovered that in days of old, when the castle was in its heyday, there were steps that led on past the front entrance – down to dungeons and a torture chamber.'

The strange residents of the old Rocky hospital

It's been pulled down now,' Beryl told me, and not before time, according to many. There are too many odd stories to tell of paranormal activity there; in fact I know someone who told me once that as he left the Rockhampton (Queensland) Base hospital after visiting a relative, he was bodily picked up and hurled to the ground. 'I'd walked only a few paces beyond the door when I was picked up and thrown down – it must have been a distance of two or three metres, and it was witnessed by a lady, who asked me if I was all right. As it turned out, I was – but I can tell you,' Rob said, 'I didn't trip or stumble. Something picked me up bodily and chucked me onto the pavement.'

As a matter of fact, I remember the Rockhampton Base hospital quite well. I was the Presbyterian minister at Gladstone, 110km to the south of Rocky, and one of our sons had his tonsils out in that hospital. From time to time I visited Gladstone people who were sent there for treatment by their doctors.

During the transition period from the old hospital to the new, the old hospital's medical ward was used for about two years as a day surgery ward – and it was that particular ward (2A) that reduced some of the staff to a state of terror.

Beryl was a nurse there and she knew what it was like to feel a nervousness akin to terror that had nothing to do with anything belonging to this world. She and many other staff members believed that the ward was haunted.

When it became a temporary day surgery, most of the patients went home not long after 3.00pm, but it was from then until about 9.00pm that whatever it was 'came to life' (so to speak). There were always at least some staff there until 9.00pm, preparing it for the next day. Sometimes the cleaning staff came after 9.00pm but none of them would go into ward 2A alone. The cleaning staff reported seeing what appeared to be the reflections of invisible feet on freshly polished floors as some invisible entity made its way across the ward. Buzzers went off in completely empty rooms. Televisions that had been left in the ward for hire when it was a medical ward suddenly switched themselves on, then some time later just as suddenly switched themselves off. Odd noises from seemingly nowhere broke suddenly into the stillness. Reports were put in.

Complaints were made. The hospital sent plumbers and electricians to investigate the oddities. Nothing unusual was detected. Beryl told me that what made her very nervous was the occasional sound of Cheyne-Stokes breathing, getting louder and louder – then suddenly stop. I must confess that sent a real shiver down my spine. Cheyne-Stokes breathing is associated with various ailments, such as sleep-apnoea, and often occurs, but not always, not long before death. Most who have sat by the bed of a dying person would know what it is and certainly all medical and nursing staff would recognise it... the laboured breathing that suddenly stops, then just when it seems it can never start again, it does. It may go on for a long time. It can be very hard for a family to endure, waiting by a bedside for the end to arrive.

I suppose, in a way, here in the quiet of the room, with the muted moan of the wind around the old building outside, and the fire casting dark, flickering shadows on the walls inside, it may not have been the best time to talk about these things, and I note you've gone a little quiet. I hope you aren't feeling nervous.

Thinking about that, I can add a little something at the end, that may, or may not, make you smile. It depends on your sense of humour.

I recall, many years ago in a small country town where I was the minister, sitting alone by the hospital bedside of an elderly patient whose condition was leading to his rapidly approaching demise. The doctor told me the man had no chance of surviving his illness.

Outside the room sat his family, who could not stand another moment of that terrible breathing. Attached to him was the heart monitor – quite primitive, I suppose, compared to the sophisticated equipment they use these days. As I listened, I watched the little bouncing ball making its way steadily across the monitor – when suddenly it stopped. I think my own heart did too, for a moment or two. The patient's eyes appeared to have glazed and when it seemed obvious he had died, I called in the doctor, who had been busy in another part of the hospital. He came in, checked for signs of life and found none. 'He's gone,' he told me; 'you can call in the family now.'

I made my way out to the waiting room and informed the family that it was over, and then led them in a prayer, thanking God for the life of that man who had meant so much to them all.

In a way, they were relieved, for they'd been told his condition was terminal, and so it was no more than a time of waiting for life to cease. I opened the door to the room and motioned them to enter. As they did so, I heard a sudden little scream from the man's wife and hurried to investigate. Beyond all odds, I heard the familiar beep – beep of the heart monitor, and saw the little bouncing ball, again making its way steadily across the screen. I stared in disbelief, then rushed off to find the doctor, who came rushing back with a nurse…

The last time I saw that former 'dying' patient was at our farewell from that town a year or so later. He sat, grinning at me from one of the seats in the hall, sandwich in one hand, cuppa in the other. For all I know, he may still be alive, perhaps dining out on his unusual story.

Ghostly footsteps in the old RPA

What is it about hospitals that seems to retain the interest of those who once worked there or were patients there, and who have since died? Come to think of it, I suppose there are few places more likely to be subject to hauntings than hospitals, where there has always been an undercurrent of emotions, ranging from numb resignation and grief, to fear – even terror – on to relief and joy at good news.

When it comes to hospitals, the most prevalent reports refer to ghostly nurses whose commitment to their selfless calling seems to extend beyond this life. I can think of more than one account, so here is one of them:

Sharyn, a friend of ours, told me a strange tale of a time when a relative was in the old Royal Prince Alfred, Sydney, as a patient, at the time when it was being pulled down to make way for the new RPA. She told me that a lot of it had already been pulled down and only one ward was in use at the time.

Sharyn and her sister went to Sydney to visit the relative who was in that last ward still being used. During the course of the visit, the patient told them that the ward above hers, which was unused and stripped of furnishings, was supposed to be haunted. Over time, tales had been told by folk who had reported seeing the ghost of a nursing sister, and even hearing her footsteps. 'I hear the footsteps quite often,' said Sharyn's family member, 'usually at night, in the ward above this one, although I know no one can be there. In fact it's been closed.'

Sharyn and her sister were intrigued and after the visit was over, decided to pay a surreptitious visit upstairs to see what they could see, so they did. When they went in, it was obvious that no one was there. The ward was completely bare. Everything had been removed and all they saw was one large, empty room.

As they stood there, suddenly they heard it – the sound of footsteps, walking across the room at about the gait one sees nurses in hospitals going about their duties. The thing was, they heard the footsteps which passed close by them, but there was no visible body attached. Sharyn said she felt her scalp tingle at the time. There was no way it could be any earthly person. It seems that the old nursing sister, if she was the invisible owner of the footsteps, was still faithfully doing her rounds around her invisible patients.

Visitations

3

My mother visited me from beyond the grave

The following story is told by LS, in her own words. I have known her all her life. She is devout in her Christian faith and in my opinion would not be capable of concocting a story like the following, some time after the death of her mother:

'I was resting on my bed, not thinking of anything in particular; entranced as usual by the beautiful gum tree that stood outside my bedroom window, where I could see birds frolicking and singing in the leafy boughs. Suddenly, out of the blue, my earthly surroundings had vanished. I felt no fear or anxiety; in fact I felt quite content and very much at peace.

In a flash, standing before me, was my darling mother. She wasn't the aged and sickly lady she was when I last saw her. She was middle aged, and dressed in a maroon costume. She looked so radiantly happy, smiling that same gentle smile that was meant only for her children and her grandchildren.

I was so overjoyed at seeing her again.

I tried to leap into her arms, but couldn't move a limb. I was completely paralysed. I tried desperately to call out to her, but I had no voice. I helplessly smiled at her and mouthed, the words 'I love you!' 'I love you!' and kept repeating it over and over again.

In an instant she warmly responded, 'I love you too!' 'I love you too!'

Then my mother was weeping, her head buried in her hands.

Desperately I tried to break loose to comfort her; but the next thing I knew, I was back in my own earthly environment. I was so overjoyed at seeing my mother so young and happy, but mystified and deeply saddened, by the sudden emotional change. Was she missing us?

Lachlan: *I'm sure she was, LS, and one day you'll see her again. Keep the faith.*

The boy who came back to reassure his mother

Many know the tragedy of losing someone near and dear, years before the age we expect them to go. It's an added tragedy to lose our children, so when Molly's son Jack, an only child and a teenager, died suddenly, she was overwhelmed by grief. The tragedy happened in a town where I was the Presbyterian minister. Her husband, Carl, seemed to be able to deal with his grief, but Molly was inconsolable.

I conducted the funeral, and for the next two or three weeks visited the bereft family regularly. I started to become very concerned for the boy's mother because she did not seem to be able to make any progress, grief-wise. She was locked in a deep valley of sorrow and tears, and there seemed to be no way out. It began to affect her health.

Then one day, it happened. When I knocked on the door of the family home, it was flung open by Molly and it was obvious something astonishing had happened, for her expression was nothing less than joyous.

She sat me at the kitchen table, and she was smiling. Her words were full of joy: 'My son came back to me last night!' I stared at her uncomprehendingly.

'Last night,' she explained, 'I had a dream – but it was so much more than a dream – a sort of vision. I can't fully describe it, but there he was. You'll understand when I tell you he was as large as life!

He was smiling at me. 'Mum,' he said, 'Stop grieving for me! I'm OK! I'm fine!'

'After that,' Molly continued, 'I drifted off into a natural sleep, and this morning when I awoke, all the sorrow and pain I'd known over the past weeks had lifted. My son is where he is, somewhere on the other side of this life, but he came back to tell me he was well. I'll miss him, but I'll grieve no more.' As far as I know, she never did.

A grandfather's Reassurance

I've known Robyn Jane all her life. She is as honest as the day, and the following account is the only incident like it that she's ever had.

It happened some time after the birth of her second child. Grief and post-natal depression is a bad combination.

'Not long after the birth of our second child, my mother rang to tell me that my paternal grandfather had suffered a severe stroke. He was in hospital and was not expected to live. We are a close family, and I loved my Grandpa.

To make matters worse, my husband and I lived in Queensland, and my grandparents lived in Moree, NSW.

That night, I had what I can only describe as a dream, but more vivid than any I've ever had. In the dream, I went to the hospital to see Grandpa. As I sat beside him I could see that he was wearing a brown suit, and was wearing a hat. In the dream it didn't occur to me that his clothing was not exactly hospital attire!

Grandpa looked at me and smiled. 'Don't worry,' he said, 'everything will be fine.'

The following morning my mother rang to tell me that Grandpa had died during the night. I was very upset, and related the strange dream to her.

She was astonished. 'There's no way you could have known,' she told me, 'but he asked to be buried in his brown suit.'

A mother brings peace from beyond

Joel is a down to earth, capable person whom I've known for some years. As with all the others whose stories are related here during our fireside chat, he's not one to believe in, or recount, fanciful stories. In fact Joel is one of the most practical people I know, so when he related his story, I was genuinely surprised. He told me that even some of his own family didn't realise what he went through after his mother died of cancer. In fact there aren't many people who know the following story, but he agreed that it's so unusual, it should be shared.

He was one of those whose grief manifested itself in anger. It's well-known that there's a fine line separating the two, and over the years I've known a number of people – mainly funeral directors and clergy, as well as an occasional doctor, who have felt the brunt of someone's anger, and I too was abused once, for no apparent reason, and told I was a liar on another. (When I was in the Army. The accuser thought I knew more than I was telling). Anger is something grief counsellors are familiar with. Anyone likely to encounter grief professionally is aware of it, and I remember learning about the correlation between anger and grief during my training for the ministry.

Joel told me that when his mother was diagnosed with cancer and it became evident she was going to lose her battle to live, he became angry, but could not understand why he felt angry towards her. He never told her how he felt. It was a terribly difficult time for him, for he loved his mother and was embarrassed and upset by his anger. He knew she couldn't help what had happened to her. Like any middle-aged, healthy person who had a loving family and a lot to live for, she didn't want to die at that stage in her life.

When finally she died, the anger continued, unexpressed, unabated, but with another prong to it. He wanted a sign from her, while at the same time recognising the incongruity of it. She was dead. How could she give him a sign?

Later in the year, on August 12, he celebrated his birthday – but 'celebrated' was not a word he used. He went to bed as usual that night – but it was a night he would never forget.

'I had an astonishingly vivid dream,' he told me, 'in which I saw my mother, as clearly as I'm seeing you. She was seated at a table, with people I didn't know. Maybe they were relatives who had died and were with her on the other side. Even in that dream-state, I knew she shouldn't have been there – she was dead. She looked at me and smiled, and her eyes were full of love.

'Is everything OK?' she asked.

I reached out to touch her hand – and suddenly I awoke, in tears, but a great sense of peace had descended on me.

I looked at the clock. It was exactly 12.03am.

The next morning I rang my father to tell him of the dream.

He listened. 'What time did you say you had the dream?' he asked.

'It was exactly 12.03am. My birthday had just gone.'

'No, it hadn't.'

Yes, it had – it was just after midnight.'

'Son, listen. You were born on August 13. Neither your mother nor I wanted you to have a birthday on the thirteenth of the month, so we asked the doctor if it would be possible to record the time of your birth a few minutes earlier, on August 12, and he agreed, for there wasn't much in it – a matter of minutes.'

'Well then, when was I born?'

'You were born on August 13, at 12.03am – the exact time of your dream last night.'

Joel smiled at me. 'I believe my mother came back to me, just briefly. Her love shone through. After that, I could release her, to live my life, free from anger and free from the guilt that came with it. She gave me closure and she gave me peace of mind. There's no better gift she could have given me.'

It's one of the most touching stories one could ever hear, Joel – thank you. Here is something else to consider about the power of love:

Love never fails. But where there are prophecies, they will cease, where there are tongues they will be stilled, where there is knowledge, it will pass away... now we see but a poor reflection; then we shall see face to face. Now I know in part; then I shall know fully, even as I am fully known. And now these three remain: faith, hope and love, but the greatest of these is love. 1 Corinthians 13:8,12-13.

A message from Nan

John's maternal grandmother, known to the family as Nan, died in hospital in 1971. Her husband had died years before.

Just before Nan died, her deceased husband visited his daughter (John's mother) who was awakened by her deceased father who said to her, 'Your mother needs you.'

John's mother dressed hurriedly and went to her room, where she discovered that her mother had just suffered a major stroke, from which she never recovered.

A story from Thailand

Here is another letter from my pile by the chair, written by a delightful girl whom I will call Trish, who is Thai. We have known Trish for some years now, and a gentler, more loving soul would be very hard to find. She now lives in Australia, and she and her husband are attending a Church, where Trish is exploring the Christian faith.

'The Mystery sound that was not so mysterious'

Nearly twenty-five years ago, my Nan, Nuen, passed away at the age of 74. Her funeral took place three days after her passing.

In late 2002, my mother and I went to Samutsakhon, one of the provinces in Central Thailand where I was born, for a holiday, where we stayed at my aunt's place.

During our stay, I prayed, offering my respects to my Nan and declared that I would make a dedication to her at the temple. In the Buddhist culture, to make a dedication means that the one who is to dedicate goes to the temple to make a donation, offering food & flowers to the monks. It is through them that those who have passed can receive gifts from the living. Buddhism in Thailand is strongly influenced by traditional beliefs regarding ancestral and natural spirits, which are incorporated into Buddhist cosmology.

Early one morning around 2.00am I awoke from a very restless sleep, feeling strangely alert. Suddenly I heard a distinct tapping sound, rather like fingers tapping on a wooden floor or table. At first I thought it was simply a sound from outside the house, but then realisation dawned: I knew I was listening to the same sound my Nan used to make when she was still alive, as she sat on the wooden bench outside on the verandah, tapping away on the wooden seat with her fingers. As I listened that morning I began to feel rather fearful, for I knew she was present, close by. My mother, who was in the same room, told me she heard the sound too.

I then remembered my vow to make offerings at the temple, which I was yet to do. I knew that the tapping was from my Nan, reminding me of my promise to her.

Later that morning, I went to the temple to make my donation and offerings, and from that time on, never heard the tapping sound again.

That mystery sound was not so mysterious after all!

The brother who came to say goodbye

My friend of many years, Ianrob, recalls a story his maternal grandmother used to relate concerning her brother, whose name was Alwyn. The year of the incident was 1929, when the old couple lived in Alexandria, in Sydney.

Very early one morning, Ianrob's grandparents were in bed and just stirring to greet the day when the blinds in the bedroom suddenly moved.

When they looked, they were startled to see a figure standing there whom they immediately recognised as Alwyn. He spoke to them, and although Ianrob can't remember the exact words he spoke, he remembers his grandmother telling him that her brother Alwyn had come to say farewell.

Some time later, they learned the news that they were almost certainly waiting to hear: Alwyn had died in Dubbo about the time he had appeared to his sister and her husband.

... and other true stories

Unexplainable, inexplicable

4

'You'll never take me alive...'

John's great uncle Bill lived in Hindmarsh in SA and was a gold prospector. He had a little shack at Mylor, SA, which he used when prospecting.

One evening he was at his shack, preparing his evening meal when, looking out through the opened door he saw a man dressed in hat and overcoat, peering in at him. They stared at each other for a brief time before the stranger turned and without a word, left.

John's great uncle was intrigued enough to watch him as he walked away, across a hill and out of sight.

A week later, the police called, seeking a man whose appearance and clothing resembled the man uncle Bill had seen. Uncle Bill told them of the man who'd visited him the previous week.

The police followed the direction the stranger had taken when he'd left the shack, where they found his body some distance away. He'd been dead at least two weeks.

The leaving of 'Taradale'

'Leaving 'Taradale,' our farm was hard,' Angus told me one day as we sat with him and his wife Barbara in the kitchen of their new home, 'for it had been in the family for one hundred and fifty years - since 1861. Barbara and I are getting on, our children all have their own careers, and no one in the family wanted to farm it. It was time to go. At least we know the person we sold it to will look after it the way we have. We've known him for years and he's always loved it.'

'Taradale'... it's a lovely name,' I said; 'where does it come from?'

'It's named after Tara, in Ireland, where the ancient kings of Scotland were crowned. It's not widely known, but away back in the past, Ireland and Scotland were known as Scotia.'

... and other true stories

I've known Rev Angus Ewin and his wife Barbara for a long, long time. Angus to this day is well-known throughout the Presbyterian Church. He was ordained in 1963 and has served in many areas of the state of NSW and beyond. He was Moderator of the NSW Assembly of the Presbyterian Church and is a man that people listen to. Two of his brothers are also ministers. The Ewin family is well represented in the Church.

A few folk we know used to go up to 'Taradale' at shearing time to help with the shearing.

Janet and I visited Angus and Barbara some years ago, at 'Taradale' near Blayney. It is a lovely property. The homestead is very old but was very well-kept and maintained, and behind it were the various sheds one finds on farms. The old laundry (not used for many a long year) was fascinating, for it was just as it must have been the best part of a hundred years ago. Barbara, Angus's wife, knew exactly who'd owned many of the objects, going back decades. It was a year or two after our visit that the Ewins left.

As we sat chatting to Angus and Barbara in their new home, he told me a story that really made me sit back and think.

'It was the day we left 'Taradale' forever,' Angus said. 'It was a bright, warm, sunny day, without a hint of a cloud in the sky. Two of the boys – our son in law and a grandson, had taken the last of the rubbish to the tip and we were due to leave as soon as they got back. We picked up our personal belongings and walked out of the house for the last time. Imagine our surprise to find ourselves in the middle of a fine mist! Not only was it the wrong time of the year for a mist or fog - it was the wrong sort of day! We were completely 'myst-ified' if you'll forgive the pun. We could see that it was over the house and the sheds but it was too thick for us to see beyond that. There was a still, heavy sort of an atmosphere in the mist too - it was very strange.

Suddenly, it lifted, and we could see the surrounding country, but no sign of mist anywhere. Just then the boys drove in. 'Did you see any sign of a mist, or fog?' I asked, when they got out of the ute. They looked at us blankly. 'Fog? Mist? Nope. It was as clear as a bell all over the valley. No sign of any fog, or mist.'

'I've spent a lot of time, thinking about that strange incident,' Angus told me. 'The mist must have been just over the house and sheds and nowhere else. I've wondered ever since if all the old relatives who had lived there over the past one hundred and fifty years, somehow congregated here, and that mist was their farewell to Taradale. I rather like to think it was something like that.'

I do too, Angus. *Generations come and generations go, but the earth remains forever.* Ecclesiastes 1:4.

'I saw a man who wasn't there...'

Many years ago, John's father was asked to take a photo of friends; a man and his wife whom he'd known for some time.

The photo was to be semi-formal, with the woman seated and her husband standing at her side. John's father obliged, and took the photo as requested.

When it was developed, it appeared to be of a woman seated in a chair. There was no indication that there was anyone by her side.

John's father was naturally astounded, and even more so when he heard the reason. The couple told him that he, the husband, failed to appear in any photo taken of him. They could only presume there was some component in his physical make-up that apparently made him invisible to the light necessary for photos. I know that this story takes us to the edge of belief, and some will find it impossible to believe, but I know John very well, and if he trusted his father to tell his son the truth, so do I.

When John told me this story, I wondered idly if something the man was holding would appear, such as a baby apparently suspended in mid-air, or a floating glass of ale or cup of tea.

It's interesting to note however that there are other, similar stories that have emerged over the years, but this one is the only one that I have heard where the story is not of some vague person whom no one has ever met. This story is from one who was there.

The clock that stopped when it shouldn't have

A lady I know whose name is Joan told me the following strange little story and it made an impact on me, because I too have an unusual clock story. When it comes to mechanical things like clocks that refuse to work when they should, or insist on working when they shouldn't, we are getting to the edge of the boundary of belief – but these things happen, and all we can do is admit we have no idea why; not, of course, forgetting the possibility that there may well be a logical explanation that we have failed to understand. Both Joan's and my stories are connected, in a strange sort of way, to the old song *My Grandfather's Clock*.

I am sure in regard to Joan's and my story that follows, many people will go for the latter explanation. Still, in this life, we should never deny possibilities beyond our own understanding.

Here is Joan's story: 'A couple of years after my husband and I moved to a small country town in western NSW, my mother passed away. She and my father had been married for fifty-four years.

Among their family treasures was a lovely mantle chiming clock which dad's mother had given them as a wedding present

The day my mother died, the clock stopped working and no one could get it going again.'

The clock that started when it shouldn't have

Not long before my retirement from St Andrew's Manly NSW, Jan, a very kind member of the congregation, gave me a farewell present. She and her husband had owned an antique shop before his death, and she had kept the clock that had been for sale, and never sold. It is made of brass, and is, (someone told me) French provincial. The clock itself is held by a small boy who looks like one of those statues of Greek mythical origin and in all it stands sixty centimetres high. It is a handsome timepiece, and needs to be wound once a week.

Some time after I retired, the clock stopped. It had been wound up but refused to go. Daunted at the thought of the expense of having an antique clock repaired, I left it sitting silently in my study for possibly three years.

Now what I am about to tell you may sound really strange, but it's the truth. One day I brought home a boxed set of CDs: 'The Music from the 1930s.' Among the lovely songs I'd seen a lovely old favourite of mine, *My Grandfather's Clock* and that was possibly why I bought the set. I remember learning it at school and I am certain most people would know of it, even if vaguely. I could hardly wait to play it on the CD player in my study; a beautiful rendition, sung by a male voice choir. The song finishes: *But it stopped, short, never to go again, when the old man died.*

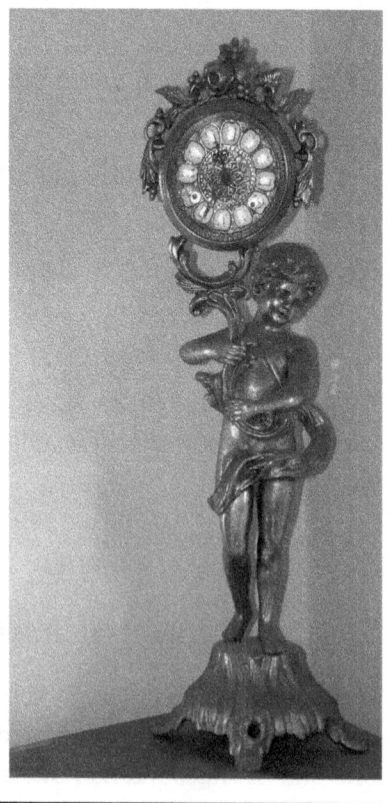

As it played I became aware of an unmistakable sound: 'ding-ding-ding-ding.' The clock that had not gone for a number of years, was striking the hour!

I was astonished, and rushed in to fetch Janet, so that she could hear it ticking away merrily, and chiming the passing hours.

My clock started when it should

have remained stopped, and Joan's mother's clock stopped when it should have kept going.

My brass clock stopped a week later, when it wound down, but what had happened so amazed me that I took it to an antique clock repairer in Newcastle and had it repaired. It was expensive, but worth it. It's been going now for the past few years, and each week on the same day, I faithfully wind it.

Now, should you ever be passing our home 'Puddleby on Sea' call in, and ask to see the miracle clock.

Merle's Story

'When I first arrived in South Africa in 1984 from Zimbabwe, I rented a flat in an area called Woodmead. One night some time later I awoke, screaming. As I sat up I saw two shrouded figures at the end of the bed, the taller of the two holding out a hand toward me. As I watched, the figures moved to the bedroom door and slowly faded away. I, strangely, thought nothing about this, had a drink of water and went back to sleep.

The next day however, I awoke feeling very tired, and when I arrived at work, one of my colleagues asked if I was okay, because I was very white and looked as though I had been drained of blood. I said I was fine and just felt very tired. The feeling of tiredness remained for about a week, but each day I felt better and began to get some colour back into my face and body.

Since then, I have not had any further recurrence of the tiredness; nor a sighting of the two figures.

 My second experience was more recent, and occurred in France at the beginning of 2008. By that time I was married. Norman and I were visiting his son and family, who live in a place called Annecy in France, very close to the Swiss border.

It is a strange town, for they have what they refer to as the 'old' town and the 'new' town.

The old town reminded me of the film *Oliver*, with lots of cobbled streets, grey stone walls and numerous alleyways which led all over the place. There was also a very old prison – no longer used, thank goodness, surrounded by a small moat. The prison had slit windows, which must have been very distressing for the people inside.

Whilst walking through the streets of the old part of town, I felt as though hands were touching me but when I looked around, there was nobody there, but I could feel a coldness – mind you, it was the middle of winter with an outside temperature of about -8°c!! I could also hear a noise which sounded almost like people wailing and yet it was not loud, and nobody else in the street seemed to hear it. I became very aware of a person around me – a lady in a grey-brown, long dress with a dirty apron and mob cap - she was never clear to my vision, but just seemed to be there.

We were in that area for only about four days, and then left to come home to Australia. For several months after we had returned, I still had a very uneasy, anxious feeling, and in the end, telephoned a lady who was a medium. She talked me through the situation and then asked me to do some visualising of the exact place where it had occurred, and discussed with me how to get rid of the feeling.

The feeling still remained with me for some days, but slowly a sensation of calm began to return, and I am now able to talk about the incident without any great feeling of anxiety.

I have tried briefly to find out whether the centre of the old town of Annecy was perhaps where people were beheaded by the guillotine, but because the situation made me feel anxious, I have never followed it up and am content to let it rest.

The piano that moved

Robina told me this one: 'Several years ago I worked as a nurse at an aged care facility, in the dementia wing. I often did the evening shift alongside another nurse called Mel. She cared for the patients upstairs and I looked after the patients downstairs. The downstairs end of the building was L shaped and the lower back corner of the wing was well known for its spooky atmosphere, especially at night. Quite a few staff had reported ghostly sightings in that back corner, and I myself had seen glimpses of things out of the corner of my eye.

One night, after I had given the residents their evening meal and medications, it was time to put each of them to bed. This took a fair while until finally I had only one resident left to see to, a lady called Maggie. Her room was in the lower back corner of the dementia unit, next to a big old piano. The piano had been donated to the dementia ward by an elderly resident, who had since passed away.

I found Maggie, who was wandering around the ward, and walked her past the piano into her room. I had just finished settling her into bed when I heard a very loud, creaking sound that certainly wasn't my nurse's back. I couldn't imagine what it could be. I opened the door and was shocked to discover that the old piano was sticking out at a 45 degree angle from the wall. That's what the creaking sound had been! I tried to move it back against the wall, but it was too large and heavy; made more difficult to move because it sat on thick carpet.

I rang Mel upstairs who was surprised when I told her what had happened. She came down and we tried with all our might to push it back, but it wouldn't budge.

It was a total mystery. How could the piano have moved? All the residents were in bed and were far too elderly and frail to move it, even if they tried. Mel and I were the only staff on the premises. Even if somehow someone managed to get in from outside, why would they do that, then sneak out? It didn't make sense.

The next day the piano was moved back into position by the handyman.

That was a long time ago. Since then I have changed jobs and moved to a different city. I can remember that night clearly though, and still can't come up with a logical explanation as to how the piano moved on its own. There are just some things that can't be explained!'

As Robina remarked, there are indeed some things that just can't be explained away, and that applies, not only to the supernatural world but to the world of science too. Sometimes I have the feeling that science (or more accurately I suppose, some scientists) seeks to explain away things that really lie outside the sphere of science and should belong more in areas such as theology or philosophy. Medical people have told me that sometimes a patient will ask them a question that has nothing to do with medicine.. It's usually a theological question such as 'Do you think there is a God?' The one asking the question apparently assumes that the doctor, by reason of his medical qualifications, can supply an authoritative answer.

In ancient times, the Gnostics had a reputation for having that sort of authority. Gnosticism was a Greek religion and the word 'gnosis' means 'knowledge.' The Gnostics had the knowledge, their devotees believed, and what they declared to be true, was true. They declared for instance that Jesus couldn't have died on the cross and had magically swapped places with Simon of Cyrene, (Luke 23:26), and it was he who died on it, while Jesus was among the crowd, laughing at Simon's fate. Odd? That's only a part of it. The opening verses of the first chapter of John's Gospel refute the Gnostic claims concerning the person of Jesus by telling the world just Who He is.

One modern scientific problem I read of recently has the scientists stymied. Apparently, according to the scientists, there aren't enough atoms to hold the universe together – it seems it should collapse in on itself. They realise that there must be something to support the universe, so they call it 'dark matter' without knowing what it is. Imagine a cake that's being made without enough flour. You pull it out of the oven and it falls to bits. That's what the universe should do.

Well, that's my pathetically inadequate description but by and large, I think it's true enough. In time of course I am sure the scientists will work it out, but it is such a complex problem it has defied the world's great scientific minds for a long time.

What does that tell me? It tells me that there is no way the universe could be formed by random chance. If you want a really wonderful story, read 'The Language of God – a scientist presents evidence for belief' by Dr Francis Collins, a physician and geneticist, former atheist, now devout Christian. He's the scientist who was the leader of the human genome project (DNA).

Now I've prattled on for ages. I hope you haven't fallen asleep. Allow me to stoke up the fire...

Done... The room was cooling down a bit. I can see rain falling outside. This big wingback chair is so, so comfy. Did you know that the 'wings' that stick out on either side were put there in olden days to prevent any wayward draft from ruffling great, great grandfather's waxed moustache, which protruded on either side of his face? Well, that's what someone told me. No need to laugh...

Now here's a fascinating little story that's another of the inexplicable stories dotted right through my long discourse... It's Robina again:

'When I was twenty-two and 'in between' houses, I stayed with some friends for three months while I looked for a place to rent. Their house was large and old and my bedroom was closest to the lounge room.

I hadn't been there long before I began to notice unusual occurrences at night. Most nights I would see tiny little orb-like lights that would dance through the dark near my bed. One night I was lying facing the wall when I heard footsteps approaching the bed. As I lay there petrified, I felt something brush my cheek. The final straw came on the same night, when a large hanging Daffy Duck picture began thumping against the wall on its own. I flew out of bed and into the lounge room and spent the night on the lounge. I was too unsettled to spend another night in that room, so spent the remainder of my stay in the house sleeping on the lounge.

Not long after I moved into a house of my own and was again able to sleep peacefully. Looking back it was an interesting experience, but you couldn't pay me to sleep in that room again!'

Some people seem to attract the attention of spooks, Robina.

Gallipoli 1990: Did God have a hand in this?

Early in 1990, on my second posting to the Australian Army Aviation Centre, Oakey Qld, the Principal Chaplain Army, Ernie Sabel, rang to ask me if I would be prepared to accompany 58 original Anzac (Gallipoli) veterans back to Gallipoli. There was, Ernie explained, to be a special service at Anzac Cove for the 75th Anniversary. Naturally, I was delighted to accept.

The PC went on to explain that the Prime Minister would be there, as well as a large contingent of all sorts of people, including many politicians, but including as well doctors and nurses and mountains of medical equipment, to reduce as far as possible the likelihood of any deaths of the old veterans, seventy-five years after escaping with their lives the first time. There was a great deal of risk involved for them anyway, for their ages ranged from a youthful 93 to a 'getting on in years' 103.

When we left Australia's sunny shores in mid-April 1990 on Qantas flight 1915 *Spirit of Australia* I still had no idea of the magnitude of the undertaking, although I realised it was very large.

Upon arrival in Istanbul, Turkey, we were greeted by Turkish soldiers, armed with automatic weapons, armoured vehicles and other indications of a military operation in progress. 'Hullo!' I said to myself, 'don't tell me we've been lured here by the Turks to finish off what we started in 1915!' (Let me hasten to add here that it was in jest that the thought crossed my mind). The Turks were most gracious and kindly. We were told that apparently at that time there were up to eight terrorist groups operating somewhere in Turkey, and our hosts were making sure we were safe, in case any terrorist group decided our arrival posed a wonderful opportunity for a bit of publicity.

If I rambled on about all the adventures I had during that time at Gallipoli, we'd be here until dawn, and we'd run out of wood for the fire. It was an unforgettable time, especially those days leading up to Anzac Day, when we rested the old warriors. They were so funny, and such characters. They were men apart. Of course they are all now gone.

We were taken by bus around the many battle fields of Gallipoli. In the photo (page 71) I can be seen chatting to an Australian Army Transport Corps corporal (who is wearing camouflage uniform) in a reconstructed trench at Chunuk Bair; a place of terrible slaughter in 1915.

I'd like to tell you briefly however of the 103 year-old, John McLeary. Unfortunately he forgot the instruction not to drink the water at a certain hotel where we were camped for a couple of days, and ended up with what the troops were calling 'The Turks' Revenge.' He wasn't the only one either. His age, of course, was against him, and for a while it was thought he may not survive. As I sat by his bedside he whispered to me 'Padre, I want you to pray that I will recover from this, and return to Gallipoli. There are some old comrades lying there at Lone Pine I want to see, before I join them on the other side.'

We had our little prayer, and he did survive, and returned safely to Australia, but it wasn't so long after that of course that he died.

I'll never forget his courage and humour, and the same applies to all those old soldiers who returned to Gallipoli, and Anzac Cove, and the many battlefields we visited during that time there.

It was still dark on the morning of 25 April, 1990, at Anzac Cove, not far from the Anzac Memorial. I'd travelled in the bus with the old veterans, who were led out to take their places at the very front of the dais where the service was to be held.

Countless numbers of people were there: New Zealanders, Turks, Australians, and people from many other nations, while buses brought more all the time. New Zealand and Australian soldiers, sailors and airmen were there in force.

I proudly wore my uniform on the dais. Offshore, there were Australian warships and later there would be aircraft above us.

I was to take only one part of the service and at that time I had no idea who was to lead it. I was down for a prayer that had been prepared for me to recite. In fact, all the prayers were in the same booklet, with the rest of the service.

When I'd seen the Order of Service back in Australia before we left, I'd been surprised to note that apparently it had not been drawn up by the people who, I thought, would have been approached to do it: The principal chaplains of The Royal Australian Army chaplains' Department. (RAAChD). Above the Principal Chaplains is the RACS (Religious Advisory Committee to the Services) who are civilian heads of churches, and when I mentioned to the Presbyterian member the peculiar lack of reference to the Christian faith in any part of the Service, he too was puzzled, but I heard no more.

It was puzzling indeed. After all, I reasoned, seventy-five years previously, there would have been few of the Anzac troops who would not have gone under the banner of one of the Christian denominations; so why was there no mention of the name of Jesus Christ?

After the end of the First World War, when the allies went back to Gallipoli, they found on the graves of the Allied dead, Moslem headstones. That was not done out of any disrespect; in fact, quite the opposite and was simply a way to mark the graves. The Turks were more than happy to have the Moslem markers replaced with Christian crosses.

The Turks honoured the Anzac invaders. If you are in any doubt about that, have a look at the very moving words on the memorial erected at Anzac Cove by Ataturk. It was he who led the Turks to victory in that campaign. He was the Turkish general, and his real name was Mustafa Kamahl. He was a brilliant soldier. It was he who led Turkey to many modern reforms and did away with the old system of the sheiks. He wanted Turkey to be allied to the West, rather than the East. Here are his words:

Those heroes that shed their blood and lost their lives...
You are now living in the soil of a friendly country. Therefore rest in peace. There is no difference between the Johnnies and the Mehmets to us where they lie side by side here in this country of ours...
You, the mothers, who sent their sons from faraway countries, wipe away your tears; your sons are now lying in our bosom and are in peace. After having lost their lives on this land they have become our sons as well.

As I stood on the dais, an official came running up: 'There's no one to lead the service!' he called. 'You're a padre – you can do that!'

And that, my dear friend, is how I came to lead the 75th Anzac Service at Anzac Cove, at dawn on 25 April, 1990.

There is a little more. I am so guileless it sometimes frightens me, and I am sure it frightens those unlucky enough to come within range.

When it came time to commence the service, I called to the microphone those who were taking part, and they did their bit. When it came time for my prayer, I finished with the words with which I always conclude a prayer: 'In the Name of Jesus Christ our Lord, Amen.'

At the end of the service, unsure of what to do, I closed with the Christian benediction: 'The grace of the Lord Jesus Christ, the love of God the Father, and the fellowship of the Holy Spirit, be with you all, this day and always. Amen.'

Not long after, I was introduced to the Prime Minister and his wife.

I had the distinct impression that the PM's greeting was something less than enthusiastic– not that I expected him to be effusive.

It was polite - but, I thought, barely. For all I know, that may be the way he was with everyone, although I doubt it.

It wasn't until much later that the penny dropped. (Guileless is too polite. 'Dumb' would be more appropriate).

Of course! The whole service was framed in such a way as not to offend our Turkish hosts! No wonder there was no mention of Jesus' name! No wonder one of the prayers mentioned 'The prophet' without mentioning which prophet!

I now suspect, rightly or wrongly, diplomacy over-rode religious considerations.

Well, they got the whole cartload from me, because good ol' Ness blew any possible diplomacy straight out of the water without even trying. It was completely innocent on my part, and not only am I not sorry, I'm delighted it worked out the way it did. I hope I'd have had the gumption to do exactly the same, had I realised what was the plan – always qualifying that of course, for it may not have been part of any plan at all. Perhaps it was all some oversight, but I'd be surprised if it was the case. What do you think?

If I'm wrong, then I am happy to apologise sincerely for my suspicions. Still, I have kept the original order of service, prayers, names of participants and so forth.

Our Turkish hosts were certainly not offended. They extended to me, and to us all, their gracious hospitality, and treated us with boundless courtesy and kindness. I felt very privileged to be there with them.

Anzac Day was special in another way: it was also the 103rd birthday of our dear old oldest Anzac, John McLeary, DCM. That night we celebrated his birthday in true Anzac style, in merriment and song, and many a raised glass.

I wonder if God intruded in there somehow, and the bungling Ness accidentally succeeded in providing the Christian content, despite alleged plans to keep it out? Maybe I'm simply being a bit neurotic here. Does the story belong in this book; the way God can work through human lives and history? I feel sure that none of those lying in the allied graves that morning at Anzac Cove would have been offended.

Premonitions

5

A few thoughts . . .

Afterwards I will pour out my Spirit on everyone: your sons and daughters will proclaim my message; your old people will have dreams, and your young people will see visions. Joel 2:28.

There are two ways that we know something is going to happen. The first are those times when we are at the scene, living it. Recently I was talking to a chap I know who has a private pilot's licence. He told me of an incident concerning a friend of his, who was flying an aerobatic aircraft at the time, showing another friend what it could do. He flipped the plane onto its back and was flying it upside down, when his friend became violently sick; the contents of his stomach covering the roof of the aircraft. The pilot flew on for a time, knowing what was going to happen when finally he righted the aircraft. Aware that it is usually impossible to land an aircraft while upside down without bending it and possibly its occupants, he finally flipped the plane right side up – and the inevitable happened: immediately the contents of his friend's stomach rained down from the roof upon the pair of them... That was certainly a time when both knew the inevitable would happen.

Sometimes our premonitions can be so powerful that what's about to happen can seem almost as inevitable as the above story: we know what is about to happen, without being in the situation at the time. I suspect (I don't really know but I certainly suspect) all of us have premonitions. Some may put them down to coincidences and while some may be coincidents, others may be true premonitions. Some may be vague but others so powerful as not to be denied.

How many times in the past have you thought of a person and shortly afterwards, that person arrives, or that person's name, or something connected to that person, pops up?

When those things happen time and again, I think one can assume that they are probably premonitions. This very week, as I write, I had what I am putting down as a premonition. Earlier in the week during one evening, my thoughts drifted to a friend whose health had been poor. I thought to myself that I must call the following day to check on his condition. Aware that my memory is suspect, I even wrote down a memo to remind myself to call.

I was out very early next morning on my police chaplaincy rounds and had my phone switched off because I was doing a lot of driving. Late that afternoon I checked the phone to discover a message: my friend had died at 9.00pm the previous evening. I wish I'd written down the time I'd written the memo, but I didn't. It may well have been about the time my friend died. I suspect that as we acknowledge those so-called 'coincidences' as premonitions, the more likelihood there is that our awareness will increase; at least, I think that is the case with me, but it's nothing that can be proved, one way or the other.

I have a belief that there is some element in all living creatures that goes beyond reason and knowledge and permits us to look 'around the time-corner' as it were, to see what lies ahead, waiting for us. I'm sure it's a defence mechanism in animals that can warn them of approaching danger. As far as we humans are concerned, I'm not talking about major world events, but the smaller things that happen constantly to people like you and me. Mind you, there are quite well-documented cases of premonitions of major events. One that comes to mind is the woman who had a nightmarish dream of the sinking of RMS 'Titanic' in which she claims that she saw people in the water and so on, but that sort of premonition lies well outside the scope of this little yarn. Most of the premonitions I've had over the years have been minor matters that don't rate mentioning, but one or two are worth recording.

Sometimes we have a very definite sensation that something is about to happen, either good or evil. Here's a 'good' one: At one time while I was serving as a chaplain on one of the P&O ships during a cruise, Janet and I were watching the artwork sales. (Carnival Cruises - P&O claims to be the biggest artwork dealer in the world, which I don't doubt. Each ship that leaves port has hundreds of paintings and other works on board, which are auctioned during the cruise).

Sometimes there are 'give-aways.' Several works, usually prints, are lined up to be given away to some fortunate person. The viewers are given tickets, which are then drawn out of a hat. The person whose name comes up can have a choice of the works on display that are to be given away.

On that occasion I had an extraordinarily strong premonition that Janet's name would come out of the hat. It was a remarkable sensation, that premonition. If her name had not come out, I would have been quite surprised, for the premonition was so powerful. Sure enough, her name did come out, and she chose an interesting painting, or rather, a numbered print (170/1100), by a well-known American artist, Thomas Tribby. The auctioneer told me it would normally fetch about $700.00 if one had to buy it.

When we returned home we had it framed. I Googled Mr Tribby, found his email address and wrote to him. He was a very pleasant man and quickly replied. In his email he told me the painting Janet won was a numbered lithographic print. He verified the auctioneer's assessment of its worth and offered to sell me the original, Bathers 88 which I recall was about $US 4,100.00. Regretfully, I had to decline. Each time I look at that painting, which we both like, I am reminded of that strange but very accurate premonition.

Premonition of an accident

Here is one not so pleasant... in fact it was far from pleasant... in fact it was quite nasty...

I was seventeen years of age at the time and had a 500cc single cylinder AJS motorcycle, which I'd bought from a friend for £50.00 ($100.00). It was a few years old but in excellent condition, apart from a dent in the petrol tank, result of a bingle some time in the past.

In those days, few young people could afford a car and in Leeton most of my friends had motorbikes, on which we roared around the town, resulting in the unwelcome attention of Constable Neville Bully, the local speed cop. He was a good man (had to be. He married a local) and looking back now, I know that he was more interested in saving our young lives than booking us. There was only one other small problem with the bike: the cap that held the lead from the magneto to the spark plug was missing. It would have cost the equivalent of all of five cents to replace, and taken me ten seconds to screw on, but somehow I hadn't managed to get around to it. Every now and then, when I hit a bump in the road, the lead would bounce off the spark plug, but I discovered I could lean down, grab the lead and drop it onto the spark plug while still riding the bike.

Donna was one of the local girls, blonde and attractive and the girlfriend of a friend of mine. One day she asked if I would give her a lift home on the back of the AJS. She lived on a property out of town, not so far from ours.

Of course I was only too happy to oblige. We turned off the main road and onto the road where she lived with her parents and brothers, which was a dirt road. Somewhere along the road, I hit a bump, and the lead to the spark plug bounced off. I leaned down to grab the lead but missed, and grabbed the end where it fits onto the spark plug.

In a fraction of a second my whole body became alive as thousands of volts of electricity from the bike's magneto coursed through my body and into Donna's. I had a sensation of sparks shooting out of my ears, and my hair became flaming bolts of blue fire. It was agonising. I've been told that when electricity passes through one body and into another, the second person gets a far bigger charge. I suspect it might be true, for as the imagined sparks exploded from my ears I heard a piercing shriek, while at the same time a pair of ankles shot up on either side of my head. When I looked around I could see my pillion passenger's form lying spreadeagled on the road, inert, apart from an occasional spasm as the electrical charge finally dissipated. I parked the bike and hurried back. Fortunately the dirt was soft and she was uninjured, although I gathered from her comments that the funnier side of the incident had escaped her. I think she decided to walk the rest of the way home. With the bike's engine turned off I replaced the lead and then rode back into town, where I spent the equivalent of five cents and bought a cap for the top of the spark plug

I can see by your puzzled expression that you have no idea where I am going with this. I think you've remarked before that you hope my sermons aren't as rambling. Well, as in the case of the sermons, I am getting there. Now let me get on with it…

Some weeks later, Donna asked me again for a lift home, and I agreed. I was amazed, thinking she must have a very short memory, because at the time of the previous disaster, as she sat there covered in dust in the middle of the road, her small frame still wracked by an occasional spasmodic jerk while still managing to look pretty, she told me she'd never get on my motor bike again – or even speak to me again, if she could help it. Of course she thought I'd electrocuted her on purpose.

I felt wonderfully forgiven and in that state of grace agreed wholeheartedly, promising not to electrocute her this time, because the problem had been fixed. As we walked to the bike she said suddenly, 'I'll drive this time. You owe me, after what you did to me.'

Still believing myself to be in a state of grace and overwhelmed by guilt at her accusation that I 'owed her', I weakly acquiesced.

Reluctantly, I kick-started my precious bike, helped her onto the seat and climbed onto the pillion seat. It was soon obvious Donna had little idea how to ride a motorbike, apart from getting it into top gear as soon as possible and winding open the throttle. We seemed to be going very fast along the Brobenah road, so I leaned over to see what we were doing. We were sitting on 70 miles per hour. Ahead was a bridge over an irrigation channel, which she almost hit, and I heard her laugh. As she laughed I saw (as a sort of vision) a skull with blonde hair streaming from it. Suddenly fearful, I tried to take control of the bike, but her arms were like steel rods and immovable. She'd 'frozen.' Seconds later, we crashed. I thank God to this day that she didn't die. I was in the hospital for about a month, but she was more badly injured than I was, and spent longer recuperating. She survived and in time I believe, married a local farmer and as far as I know lived happily ever after. I hope so. That was what I would call a premonition of impending disaster, but far too late to do anything about it.

I didn't want the premonition (I didn't want the accident!) but it popped into my mind just before it happened.

So (I hear you ask), are there scriptural precedents for premonitions? There certainly are– lots of them. One that springs immediately to mind is the premonition of the wise men, who followed the star to Bethlehem to offer to the Christ Child their gifts of gold, frankincense and myrrh. You may recall they'd dropped in on Herod on the way through, seeking the whereabouts of the child. Over a cuppa and a yarn (I made up that bit) they told Herod they were seeking the one who had been born king of the Jews.

The scheming Herod replied, as he stroked his hairy beard, (forgive this and the following bit of poetic licence too): 'Hmmm... how interesting! And here was I, thinking all along that I was king of the Jews – silly me! Anyway, when you find this kid, pop back in and let me know. I'll get Ishmael to fly me out in the Camelair, so that I too can bow the knee, touch the forelock, do the odd bit of grovelling. and so on...' (Ignore all that. If you want to find the true version, go to Matthew 2:1-12. That wasn't the end of the story either. Herod, when he realised he'd been dudded by the wise men, decided there was no way he was going to allow some kid to take over his patch, so set about having all male children aged two and under, killed.

Fortunately, God had already warned Joseph and Mary to get

out of town, so they legged it down into Egypt until things cooled down, naturally taking Jesus, (whom Herod was so keen to meet) with them. If this is not an example of God's intervention; a holy premonition, I don't know what is. (Matt 2:13-18).

If you are interested in learning more of the ways God is working His purposes out, the Bible is a treasure house of wonderful stories.

I am feeling a little embarrassed as I divulge all this information, fearing that, if you had suspected all along that Ness was something of a nutter, the evidence is now beyond all doubt. All the same, there may be others who don't see it quite that way... a trifle unhinged, maybe, and perhaps, on the wheel of life, in need of a wheel alignment and balance, but I want to tell you all this before the Lord calls me from this veil of tears. If I had any doubt about what I am telling you, then I would not tell you. I am not attempting to analyse but simply tell you what happened to me. They are not porkies, for one day I will have to give an account of myself. I don't think they are the product of a deranged mind, although who's to say?

The cowled lady

Let me take you back to Leeton and the farm. At that time I had a beautiful golden cocker spaniel, whose name was Casey, who slept on the end of my bed, keeping my tootsies warm during frosty Riverina winters.

There was an occasion when I had a vision of some evil manifestation that appeared in the form of someone from another age or era – perhaps somewhere early in the 19th century. (See the section 'The matter of evil').

One night there was another visitation, but this time, entirely different. It was a woman (yes, I was about 15 or so and doubtless ten million, million male hormones were raging crazily through my young body, but it was nothing like that). She was dressed completely in black, and was a hooded figure, like a monk. She did not face me. I saw her only side-on, She moved, or it seemed glided, a little, beside the bed. I had no sense of fear; on the contrary, she carried an aura of peace and gentleness. I didn't see her go. I must have drifted into deeper sleep, but it was a vivid recollection when I awoke.

Over breakfast, my mother asked, 'What was wrong with Casey? We could hear him barking and snarling. We've never heard him do anything like that before. I was just about to see what was happening, when he stopped.'

Casey was gorgeous, and placid, not given to disturbing the peace. He enjoyed a good night's sleep.

When my mother told me what she'd heard, I became aware, dimly, of hearing his barking and snarling. Normally I would have awoken. It was as if I had been in some sort of trance-like state, for I didn't stir.

Now I hear you asking, 'What has all that to do with premonitions?'

Ever since I saw that apparition, she has visited me from time to time, but only when something unpleasant is coming my way; a visible premonition of an accident; almost like a guardian angel who lets me have the accident, but so far I have survived - obviously.

The annoying thing is, she doesn't always warn me. She did not, for instance, warn me of approaching calamity that Sunday evening in 1966 when I missed a turn on the Dorrigo mountain road, on the way down to take a service at Bellingen for the Rev Rod Jepsen, who was on holiday at the time. It's a dangerous road to this day. I missed an S-bend and disappeared into space in my little Morris Major. It stopped falling two hundred feet down. That's just a bit over sixty metres. I know the distance, because the man from the garage who winched it up had to use two hundred feet of cable, told me. (There are other drops on that road, far deeper). Not surprisingly, the little Morris was a write-off. Fortunately, in those days they used to build cars made of real steel.

On another day in 1983, she was there.

I was a chaplain in the Australian Regular Army at the time and on that occasion was on an exercise with the Third Battalion, the Royal Australian Regiment (3RAR, it's called) which in those days was based at Holsworthy NSW.

I was driving a Land Rover, and while to all appearances it was a military vehicle, it was owned by the Salvation Army's Red Shield. The Red Shield works with the Army but its members are not serving personnel. The Red Shield supplies equipment and people to go out on exercises and support the troops. The soldiers love them. The Sallys have a long history in the Army, taking hot drinks and food into remote areas, including in wartime, wherever soldiers are. The Red Shield people are the Gospel with its sleeves rolled up.

I myself have had many a reason to bless them; particularly when I was a National Serviceman. Their Red Shield tents, providing hospitality, writing material, food and drink and kindly faces, was a home from home for many a homesick 'Nasho' as we were called.

Explanations over, let's hit the road again in that Land Rover owned by the Salvation Army's Red Shield, on exercise 'Aiken Victory' heading off into the wilds of Northern NSW. The date was Saturday, 20 August 1983.

Ted, the Red Shield man, was a great fellow. He loved God and he loved his work. He was compassionate and kindly and we all regarded him with great affection. He was also elderly, and told me he hated driving, so asked if I would drive his vehicle on that particular occasion. The CO was happy about that, so we set off in convoy with the rest. The company camped the first night at Tamworth showgrounds. I've never been so cold. The ice was everywhere next morning. Everything was a solid block of ice. I was too.

Well before Armidale I began to have a very uneasy feeling; the sort of feeling that defies rational explanation. It was a lovely day and all was going well; so how does one explain that sort of feeling? Ted and I were following a tanker in the convoy. The end of the tanker came to a sort of point and this one had an iron ring on the end. As I glanced at it, it became a skull for a second, then changed back to being an innocuous ring on the end of a water tanker. My heart gave a sudden lurch and I became an extra careful driver. Not long after, word came back to us that one of our vehicles had gone off the road, but there were no injuries. That was good news – no one injured but nonetheless an accident. Perhaps, I thought, that was the premonition of impending danger I'd been having. It was a good thought, but the nagging anxiety persisted – and then I saw her: the cowled lady, and I felt that stab of dread. She was in a paddock, standing there somewhere around Armidale – but when I looked again, I saw it was only a tree; a dead one at that, vaguely resembling my cowled visitor. I suspected that more was to come, so I drove even more carefully.

Some time later, the convoy turned off the New England Highway and headed down towards the coast through mountain country. The road was quite good. It was narrow, but tarred. As we swung around one bed, a landslide of tumbling rocks and dust crashed across the road right in front of us. I hit the brakes – hard. As the brakes bit, the brakeless Army box trailer I was towing; narrow, high and heavily overloaded, took over. Its sheer weight forced the Land Rover forward, out of control. The trailer, doing 360 degree rolls on the back of the vehicle, carried us to the very edge of a great drop. We ran along the side with inches to spare, knocking out white posts like ninepins. My terror doesn't bear thinking about as I fought to keep the Land Rover from going over the side, to certain death. By God's grace, the Land Rover stopped, parallel to the edge of the abyss, the left hand wheels only inches from it. I glanced at Ted. He didn't seem at all ruffled. He smiled at me and said 'It's nice to know God answers prayers. I wonder how the boys would have got on without one padre and one Red Shield man?' I had to laugh, (shakily). Ted was amazing. The next thing he did was to climb out and make me a badly needed cuppa – and for others too. Behind us, a three-ton Army truck had slewed around as it came to an emergency stop, its rear hanging out across the drop.

I was interested to read from my diary of the incident. On the top of the page dated Sunday 21 August 1983 I have written: *... but one step between me and death. 1 Sam 20:3.* Here are a couple of excerpts from my diary of that day: *It (the box trailer) began to lurch sickeningly from side to side, dragging the Land Rover with it. Tyres screamed.. we were on the point of overturning ourselves as I lost control. Terror.. hopelessness... numb despair rushed through me. We careered madly towards white posts and a mesh fence with a great drop on the other side. Guide posts rushed up as I fought for control – then crash - crash as we hit the posts. 'Oh God – we're going over!' We ran with the outside wheels along the rim of death, posts going over like ninepins. Suddenly, miraculously, we were stopped... We just sat there. We were no more than one pace from a dizzy drop...'*

(Later) ... *good old Sgt 'Bing' Crosby came over to express his concern. He was in a loquacious, expansive mood, as he was that memorable time in Malaysia. (Later again) The odd, weird thing is that I was given warnings once again of a supernatural kind, as I have been in the past... Anyway, Ted and I survived. God has work for us yet. 'Praise God, from whom all blessings flow.'* AMEN.

Sadly, however, for Ted that wasn't the end of his story. A few months later he asked me if I would be free to go on an exercise with him out west somewhere, with 2 Cavalry Regiment, also based at Holsworthy in those days. He wanted me to drive. As it turned out, I couldn't go that time and a few weeks later, word came back that Ted had rolled the Land Rover, which had an aluminium roof. It had caved in and Ted was seriously injured to the point where he spent the rest of his life in a hospice. I was deeply saddened at the news, and have since wondered if somehow the premonition I had was a warning, not for me, but through me to him. We'll never know this side of eternity. Ted *fought the good fight of faith. He took hold of eternal life.* (1Timothy 6:12).

Heather's premonition

Heather is a pleasant young woman who was a member of our Manly congregation, but has since married and moved away.

In that same congregation was a man named Ben. He was a lawyer by profession and an elder of the church. In so many ways Ben helped the church regarding legal matters that can crop up from time to time. Ben was only too happy to give his time, gratis, to his Church, and was a fine man whose full support could be relied upon always. He was always a repository of wise counsel.

Ben told me one day that he was booked in to have an operation. It was a simple enough operation: a knee reconstruction. He'd had one knee repaired and now it was time for the next one. 'I knew all those football injuries would catch up on me one day,' Ben told me ruefully.

Finally he went into hospital, had the operation and all appeared to be going well.

The following Sunday, with Ben still in hospital, Heather was on 'door duty.' That meant she was on the roster to open the door of the church half an hour or so before the service was due to commence, get all the hymn books and orders of service ready to hand out, welcome visitors and greet the regulars.

When she opened the door of the church she was surprised to see Ben standing on the footpath, looking up at the church.

She was about to greet him and ask him inside, but suddenly realised it wasn't Ben at all. Instead she saw a youngish, slim, red-headed man making his way up the hill.

'How on earth could I ever mistake that man for Ben?' she asked herself. Ben was in his seventies and of stocky build.

She thought no more about it until, with the congregation in the church and the service ready to commence, she made her way to her seat – just in time to hear me say 'I regret to announce the death of Ben... early this morning, in hospital.'

Heather was astonished, trying to absorb what she'd just seen, with what she'd just heard me say.

It was true, sadly enough. Ben had died early that morning, result of a clot that had moved. There is no way Heather could have known of his death. I'd been told only minutes before, when John Begg the session clerk told me. Ben's wife had just rung John to tell him.

Joan's premonition

Joan is a lady who lives with her husband in country NSW. She and her husband have a family (all grown up now) and are members of their church. Janet and I have stayed with them before, so know them well.

It's a fact that some people have quite a few paranormal experiences over a lifetime, and Joan is one of them. She is a farmer's daughter, grew up on the land, and is a very practical person. I have not the slightest doubt regarding the authenticity of any of her stories. If I did, regarding any stories I'm relating to you, they would not be included. These words are Joan's, from a letter received:

'One day Dad bought a bay stock horse for me to ride, and help with the stock work. We named her Kit, and she was very lively for a while; however she soon settled into her new home, and we became very good mates. One night I had a very vivid dream, in which I let her through a gateway into a smaller paddock where I usually caught her. At the other end of this catching paddock there was a dam of water, which had a fence, and wooden rails going down into the water.

She always waited for me to put the bridle on, but this morning she just galloped for the dam, swam around the rails, and ran up to the top end of the next paddock. This happened exactly as I had dreamed, and I was really stunned, as it had never happened, before, and since.'

A wife's premonition

Stories abound of those who have had a premonition concerning something that is to befall, not upon themselves, but a loved one, and the following is one such case.

Premonitions are often born out of love. Robian told me she heard God tell her of Ianrob's accident and related the story I'm going to tell you about shortly. St Paul, in his first letter to the Corinthians, chapter 13, wrote of the three great virtues, faith hope and love: 'But the greatest of these,' he writes, 'is love.'

Robian and her husband Ianrob, and Janet and I go back a long way – getting on now to fifty years, and a more sensible and practical couple than our friends it would be hard to find. Robian is a quiet and gentle person; one who seems to possess 'a calm and heavenly frame' as one the old hymns puts it, whose walk with God is a close one. Ianrob is a fellow minister, and it was through the Church that we all first met.

They, like most people, live completely normal lives, but every now and then that 'other world' breaks in upon them, as Robian relates here:

'Not long after Ianrob and I were married, I took on a teaching position at Bolwarra school in the Hunter region of NSW.

One day while in the classroom I heard the sound of sirens approaching, and shortly after an ambulance, fire engine and police car screamed past the school.

'Ianrob's had an accident!' I was overwhelmed by that certain knowledge. It wasn't a case of 'I hope Ianrob hasn't had an accident!'

I knew, as surely as if someone had stood before me and told me.

I suppose in a way it was like that, although I couldn't see Him. I knew God had told me.

I had to wait of course and sure enough, not long after, a lady from the Largs congregation rushed in with the news: 'Ianrob's had an accident!'

'I know,' I answered. She was quite taken aback, as you would imagine. 'God told me,' I informed her. I don't know whether she believed me or not, but it's true: Ianrob had been involved in a very serious road accident, and I'd known it.

Later, it emerged that Ianrob was on his way home when he suddenly remembered something he should have done. He executed a U-turn in his little VW Beetle, but another vehicle hit the back of his car, which immediately exploded in flames. Ianrob was knocked unconscious. Those were pre-seatbelt days. Ianrob had on a lap-belt, but that didn't prevent his head from hitting the steering wheel, rendering him unconscious.

The other driver jumped out of his vehicle and tried desperately to drag Ianrob free, but failed.

Fortunately and by God's grace he had a two-way radio, which he used to call for assistance, and it was that assistance that Robian saw tearing past.

The fire brigade officers managed to free the unconscious Ianrob from the wreck with only singed eyebrows and hair, but it was a close call, and he spent some time in hospital.

Robian's premonition is an amazing example of a premonition that goes beyond what we normally understand a premonition to mean. The story appears to fall more into the area of foreknowledge.

The year of Ianrob's accident was 1966. Five months earlier, as I have recorded elsewhere, I had made a slight miscalculation on an S-bend while driving down the Dorrigo Mountain road to take a service at Bellingen and had plunged two hundred feet over the side. I too had miraculously survived.

As I said to Ianrob, the Presbyterian Church went close that year to losing two of its best-looking young ministers; a comment that elicited the expected response from our wives.

If cars could talk, I am sure they would echo the words of T.L. Peacock's dramatic poem from Celtic mythology, *The War Song of Dinas Vawr*: 'We orphaned many children, and widowed many women.'

(Pass those bikkies, please... telling all these tales is hungry work).

George's story

I've known George who has been a family friend for well over forty years. We met in Coonamble during my days as the Presbyterian minister there.

We both arrived in Coonamble at the beginning of the same year; I as a minister and George as a High School science teacher at Coonamble High. He was a young, single man at the time. He was a Christian; still is, in fact, and attends his church regularly.

Back in those days I was delighted to see him at church each Sunday, occupying a seat in one of the pews. He made a number of friends around the town and district and spent quite a bit of time with us.

He wasn't a schoolteacher for long. He spent most of his career working as a scientist with the CSIRO on radio telescopes and was one of those chosen to work on the international SETI (Search for Extra-Terrestrial Intelligence) program.

George lives not far from us these days, so we see each other quite regularly. George has his feet planted firmly on the ground but is happy to acknowledge that life holds many mysteries, both this side of life and the other.

He had a strange story to tell me years ago, and I asked him about it a couple of days ago, so it arrived all fresh for me. It seems like a simple case of instinct or luck, but think about it, and you will see it is really quite complex:

Years ago, he was part of CSSM, a Christian Beach Mission organisation. Funnily enough, the committee met, not anywhere near the beach, but at someone's house away up in the Blue Mountains.

When he was asked to go to the meeting for the first time one year, he had no idea where the town was, let alone the street, and in those pre-GPS or SatNav days, he set off with only scant directions. He travelled along a ridge line in the hills for some time, and even asked directions, but no one seemed to know the place where he was heading.

As he drove along one road, not knowing where he was going, he had a strong feeling – more like a sensation, that he should turn right at another road, so he turned there. Shortly after, he had another very strong sensation, urging him to turn right again, so again he obeyed his instincts. Some time further down that road, he was struck by the incongruity of travelling along in the dark, seeking a place where he'd never been before purely on instinct, so he turned back the way he had come, until several miles later, he found a garage where he obtained directions. When he looked at the directions he realised that, if he'd gone a short distance further on – a matter of a few hundred yards, he would have found the street he was looking for.

So often, we disobey or ignore the marvellous gifts that God has given us. If we do it often enough, we lose them forever.

How do we explain such mysteries, as outlined in this and other stories? I do not know. I simply know that God has blessed us with gifts which by and large have fallen into disrepair, mainly because of lack of use, refusal to believe they exist, and the advance of technology which renders those sorts of gifts 'surplus to requirement.' Every now and then however, they surface. I encourage you to give some thought to your own premonitions in the context of God-given gifts. When we acknowledge them for what they are, I think it's a bit like training our bodies. God would not have given us these gifts if he did not want us to use them, as the scriptures make plain.

'If Only' – or premonitions ignored

The words, 'If only' are often the aftermath of premonitions we may have had but have shrugged off as fanciful, often to our regret.

(Pass another of Janet's little raspberry slices, please. How's your hot chocolate? Ta...)s I suppose quite a few of us can recall a time when those plaintive words have been wrenched from our hearts and onto our lips: 'If only...'

If you are familiar with Thornton Wilder's play *Our Town* you'll remember the anguish of those who have died, watching the interactions between themselves and loved ones that have taken place in the past. From the grave, they realise just how short is life, and once life has gone, so has any opportunity to tell their loved ones how much they love them.

In Perth, during my time in WA, there was a small group of retired chaplains from various denominations and organizations who had formed the Chaplains' Association, which met monthly at the TPI Centre for a meal and a meeting. I was given an open invitation to join them whenever I could, and I did so. I was the only one still serving, and by far the youngest, for I was a Regular Army chaplain. Some of those old-timers went back as far as World War 2, so being with them was a great source of yarns. They were the finest of men and a pleasure to be with. It was also heart-warming to observe the camaraderie they shared, regardless of denominational differences.

The Association met on the first Friday of each month, and I recall the meeting on 7 July 1989 only too well. Rev Don McCaskill arrived late, for he'd rushed back from a funeral service out in the bush, where he'd officiated at the funeral of an old friend.

I had a particular liking for Don. He was a humble, Godly man, unassuming and kindly. He'd graciously invited me to his home to meet his wife and family, and she was just like him in her warmth and kindliness. They were a very special couple.

Don certainly didn't consider himself great, but those who knew him did. One day, at one of the monthly lunches, as we sat together, he told me he had stomach-ache and was going to lie down for a while. I knew he'd had heart problems and was also aware that apparent stomach pains can disguise heart attacks. For some reason I had a distinctly uneasy feeling, but told myself that it was probably just another one of his upset stomachs. I looked at the others, but no one else appeared worried. After lunch we found him lying on a couch, and one of his old cronies said he'd stay with him until he felt better. I left and returned to Campbell Barracks.

The news came that evening. Don had died on he couch shortly after we left.

'If only...' I've often wondered why all of us that day had ignored Don's words that there was nothing much wrong with him, and not to call an ambulance. 'It's only a stomach ache,' he'd insisted. Maybe, if he'd been taken to hospital, he may have been revived. Maybe he wouldn't have died... Or maybe it was his pre-ordained time. We'll never know this side of eternity. 'If only...' words filled with meaning and emotion.

At his funeral service a few days later, I realised just what a great man he was. Much of his ministry had been out in the north-west of WA, in the country beyond the gold fields of Wiluna, where he'd become a legend in his own time, among black folk and white folk alike. An Aboriginal Uniting Church minister presented Mrs McCaskill with an Aboriginal flag, with a poem about Don in the middle of the sun.

It was a very moving and lovely service and I am sure his family was comforted. Although Don had gone to his eternal reward, what he achieved carries on: *He, being dead, still speaks* (Hebrews 11:4), which means that although he has gone, his work continues. *Yes, says the Spirit, they will rest from their labour, for their works follow them.* (Revelation 14:13).

A friend and colleague of mine told me of the time his parents called at his manse in NSW on their way around Australia. They had a caravan, and they were off to join the grey nomads. They were heading for WA.

My friend told me that when his father farewelled him and the family, he had a sudden feeling that he would never see his father again. 'It was something in his voice,' he told me; 'Something in his eyes...' He told his wife of his premonition at the time, and in time, sadly, it came to pass. His father had a heart attack and died in Esperance, WA.

When we have premonitions like that, I wonder how it would have affected our farewell; if the farewell hugs, kisses, handshakes, would have been warmer, more embracing, if we'd had a premonition we may never see that loved one again?

On a lighter note, and remembering that this yarn includes 'and other true stories,' the world-famous cellist, Mstislav Rostropovich, who died in 2007, once had an unpleasant experience that came down to a single word he uttered. The incident was recalled during an interview I listened to on ABC Classic FM before he died. I think Margaret Throsby was conducting the interview. She's a brilliant interviewer. Anyway, it seems that Rostropovich was to play at a concert in Hong Kong. At the customs counter the young Chinese lass asked Rostropovich his occupation. He replied 'Cellist.' The lass pushed a button and immediately large men descended upon the astonished musician and carted him off to prison. When the dust settled, it turned out that Rostropovich's accent, and the Chinese official's poor English, was the cause of it all. When he said, 'Cellist,' she thought he'd said 'Terrorist'!

It was finally resolved, and according to the account I heard, the British Governor of Hong Kong (still under British control at that time) was so embarrassed, he personally escorted Rostropovich back to his plane at the end of his stay.

I've often mused over that story, and have wondered if Rostropovich himself, while languishing in his prison cell, had thought to himself, 'If only I'd replied 'Musician' instead of 'Cellist,' perhaps all this may never have happened.'

'If Only...' Two fateful words with such deep implications, sometimes capturing a whimsical daydream and at other times a dark tragedy. Maybe you can think of an 'If only' that changed your life.

Those three men: my dear old friend, Rev Don McCaskill, my friend's father, and finally the great Rostropovich, have 'gone the way of all flesh' (which is a euphemism for 'they're all dead'). We'll never know, this side of eternity, what would have happened if the circumstances had been different for them; if those who had the premonitions had recognised them as such, and if Rostropovich had changed just one word.

It's all summed up in one line of an old poem by the 19th century poet Thomas Bracken that my father used to recite: 'Not Understood.'

Ah! More than this we may not question, for the truth is with the dead.

'Duck, Nils!'

Quite a few people over the years have told me they have heard a voice speaking to them from out of nowhere. Of course we understand that if we hear voices constantly, then it may be time for a chat with our friendly corner psychiatrist, for it could possibly indicate some form of psychosis. There are, however, others who may hear a voice from nowhere only once in a lifetime, and I'd like to refer you to an experience my late father-in-law told me, many years ago – a voice from nowhere, which saved his life.

Nils Gustav Rodstrom was born in Gothenburg, Sweden, on 27 May, 1906, where he spent the first fifteen years of his life with loving parents and two brothers, Carl and Targ and two sisters, Britta and Eva.

At age fifteen however, Nils, like so many young Swedes before him, went off to sea. He told me that he was supposed to start his sea-going career aboard a sailing ship, but the train to the coast was delayed and when he and his father arrived at the dock, they could just make out the masts of Nils's ship disappearing over the horizon.

He then shipped aboard a tramp steamer, as they were called in those days, where he spent the next five years of his life.

He never saw his parents again. It would be another fifty-five years before he set foot on his native soil once more, at age 70, when he went back to greet surviving members of his family and their families and introduce his Australian wife – somewhat belatedly.

Every now and then Nils recounted to me some of his adventures during those five years at sea, but one in particular stayed in my mind:

His ship docked at Cairo to pick up cargo, and that evening the crew went ashore for some entertainment. Nils was forbidden to go. He was only a boy and the crewmembers looked after him and protected him the way they would their own sons back in Sweden. Nils told me it was a hot night, and with nothing to do, he became bored. Finally, he decided to see what his shipmates were up to. He'd heard where they were heading, so somehow managed to find his way to them, where they were drinking at a bar.

When they saw him they were annoyed, and waved him away. 'Go back to the ship, Nils!' he was told; 'This is no place for a young boy!'

He did as he was told. The dock area was ill-lit, with no one around.

He felt a little nervous, he told me, so walked quickly.

Suddenly he heard an urgent call: 'Duck, Nils!' He ducked immediately. A knife whizzed over his head and embedded itself, quivering, in a crate in front of him. Instinctively he grabbed the knife, pulled it out and ran for the ship and safety.

The other crew members returned together later in the evening, in jolly good spirits after an entertaining night out. When Nils told his story, they were genuinely amazed, he said, and each denied vehemently that any of them had followed him.

'We would not have sneaked after you – we would have walked beside you,' they told him; 'and you would have had a big lecture on the folly of walking the docks of Cairo alone at night. Many a sailorman who has done that is on the bottom now... knifed, robbed, his body rolled off the docks into the sea.'

Each of us will have to make up his or her own mind regarding that story. Did one of the seamen follow young Nils? Why not walk beside him and take him back, as they told him? That would have been real protection – two walking together; not someone sneaking behind. Why the secrecy? From what Nils told me, those men were up-front types who would not dream of secretly following him, and they made that quite plain to him.

I believe they were telling the truth; not because it makes a better story but because it makes sense. I don't know about you, but it would not cross my mind to sneak after someone when I could walk beside him or her.

'Where is the knife now?' I asked my father-in-law.

He shook his head. 'I wish I knew. I had it for years and showed it to people when I told them my story. Somewhere along the line, it was lost, stolen or strayed.'

Nils had some other great stories to tell; adventures at sea, and later, at age twenty-one, going ashore at Brisbane Australia, and staying... adventures working around the Australian bush, then meeting the girl who was to become his wife, getting married, then moving to Gunnedah, and the arrival of their first child, Janet, (who was to become my wife twenty-one years later), who was followed by three more children. Then there was his dismay at discovering who was to become his first child's husband. See *A Kangaroo Loose in the Top Paddock*, by Lachlan Ness; a funny story indeed. (Ed.).

Nils became a well-known businessman in Gunnedah, but never again did he hear a voice from the other side.

Can we equate this story with scripture? The first that springs to mind is a prophecy to Zion from the prophet Isaiah 30:21 (NIV): *Whether you turn to the right or to the left, your ears will hear a voice behind you, saying, 'This is the way; walk in it.'* Isaiah 30:21.

The point I am making is that God communicates with us; sometimes through His voice, and sometimes through His messengers; for instance, the lovely story of the Nativity in Luke's Gospel, chapter 2, tells of the shepherds, minding their flocks at night when the angel of the Lord appeared and told them of the birth of Jesus in Bethlehem.

God communicates in various other ways and to various people to achieve His purposes. While in exile, God spoke to Moses from the burning bush. (Exodus 3:4ff). Abraham and Sarah had a visit from three strangers who turned out to be angels. (Genesis 18). The angel Gabriel spoke to Mary (Luke 1:26ff).

Paul heard the Lord speak to him on the Damascus Road. It was quite a dramatic incident: *'As he neared Damascus on his journey, suddenly a light from heaven flashed around him. He fell to the ground and heard a voice say to him, 'Saul, Saul, why do you persecute me?'*

'Who are you, Lord?' Saul asked. 'I am Jesus, whom you are persecuting,' he replied.' (Acts 9:3-5). There are many, many examples in scripture, and those ones just popped into my head as I spoke. Mostly, however, it's a 'still, small voice' that may come to

us in some other way we can recognise, but whatever way God's word comes to us, we know when He is communicating. A friend of mine; a minister in another denomination, lost both parents (one unexpectedly) within a little over a month. They were only in their fifties. 'I was grief-stricken,' he told me, 'and quite depressed. As I contemplated the sadness that had overtaken me, I heard, quite loudly, a voice that said very distinctly, *All, all will be well.* And it was.'

I believe my father-in-law did hear a divine voice that saved him, but if you ask me why, I can't answer. All I can say is that God, Who knows the end from the beginning, has His reasons. It could be that somewhere in the future He has plans for one of Nils's line because of some unique gift they may possess. I don't know, but I know He knows, and that's all I, or any of us, need know.

'I hear the drums, Papa, I hear the drums...'

Here is a story from the First World War:

Janet and I have a friend, Bev, and one day as we chatted, Bev had quite a fascinating story to tell about a great aunt of hers, whose name was Leila Bond, which was her married name, but when this story took place, she was only young. She lived with her parents (Bev's grandparents), Peter and Trudy Tighe, in Maitland, NSW.

Peter, Leila's father, loved poetry and enjoyed writing it. During WW1 he wrote the words of a popular recruiting song that went: *Cooee, Cooee, you're wanted at the Dardanelles.* Edward Tyrell wrote the music. Peter also wrote words for other recruiting songs.

Peter was a well-known local businessman; a stock and station agent, with his feet well and truly on solid ground, but when Leila was small it began to dawn on him and his wife Trudy that their young daughter was somehow 'different.' She was 'fey,' as the Scots would have called her; unmistakably psychic. Those qualities frequently manifested themselves in various ways, in visions and premonitions that the family found a little unnerving.

One day Leila said to her father, 'I hear the drums, Papa, I hear the drums... I think it has something to do with Uncle Joe.'

Joe Mulhall was away overseas, serving as a soldier with the AIF (Australian Infantry Forces).

'Nonsense, Leila!' her father replied; 'there aren't any drums! I can't hear any drums!'

'Yes, there are, Papa – I hear them – I hear the drums!'

Within half an hour, the dreaded telegram was delivered: the family learned that Uncle Joe had been killed in action. Leila's premonition had proved tragically correct.

... and other true stories

'Let the little children come to Me..'

6

'From the lips of children... You have ordained praise'
Matthew 21:16

From Vera Ryan

I've known Vera for quite a few years; since 1968 in fact. She was a Presbyterian Deaconess whom Janet and I met when I was in my final two years at St Andrew's United Faculty of Theology, Sydney. Vera is one of the brightest people I know and although now retired, had a brilliant career as a Deaconess. One of her last and I think most remarkable roles before retirement was as a chaplain at the Children's Hospital, first at Camperdown, Sydney, then Westmead, Parramatta, where her compassion, intelligence, sensitivity and great ability came into full play. There are countless numbers of stories that tell of her work among the children at Camperdown and Westmead.

Like most associated with the Christian Church, there is no such thing as retirement, and Vera and her husband still carry out a great work in the Uniting Church. Janet and I are very fond of her and her husband. Here is what Vera told me in a recent letter:

'When Kerry Packer fell from his horse during a polo game his heart stopped and he was clinically dead until revived by what came to be known as 'Packer Whackers.' Of interest to me was his comment regarding his 'death,' which I have paraphrased in part: 'I've been on the other side and let me tell you, there's nothing there.'

Earlier that same week one of our very young patients died, soon after telling her mother that God had told her He was coming to take her to heaven and that her mother was not to worry; she would be all right.

During my time as chaplain at two children's hospitals I heard those sorts of stories several times. There were teenagers, like Casey, who suffered from cystic fibrosis. She had been in hospital several weeks, waiting for 'brand new treatment' her doctor spoke about.

On this particular night her mother returned from the dining room to be told, 'God has told me I am going to die tonight, and I need to say goodbye to lots of people.' She said to her little brother, 'Give me a kiss'. He asked why, and she said, 'Because I'm going to die and I want a kiss!'

The word spread through the hospital and her fellow sufferers with cystic fibrosis gathered around her bed as staff members came in to say their goodbyes. Some staff members were at home but on being phoned, came in. Her doctor came in and when he arrived she said with a smile, 'There really isn't any new treatment, is there?!'

He admitted that there was not, to which she replied, 'I know - that's OK'.

As the night wore on she remembered other people she wanted to farewell, so asked for a tape recorder, which was brought to her and she recorded some personal messages.

In the early hours of the morning, supported by a fellow sufferer as she tried to breathe and with her beloved family around her, she died.

At the other end of the age spectrum, Nicholas was born with a degenerative and very rare abnormality. He was not expected to live more than 12 months. He spent a large part of his life in hospital and was not able to communicate verbally. Those who loved him however were in no doubt of his communication skills.

He had a strong spiritual sense, getting quite excited when he was taken to the family church. He had favourite hymns and would bounce in his chair when they were sung. He would show utter disinterest in others!

I used to call him 'Jesus' Boy,' and would be given his special, 'I know you,' smile. If I greeted him in any other way he would turn his face away and purse his lips until I greeted him correctly. Then that special smile would shine out. Only those he especially loved were recipients.

Nicholas achieved so many 'unattainable' goals: he went home for long periods; with the help of a frame he stood up; he went to preschool; he celebrated his 4th birthday.

At Christmas time his mother told me that she knew this would be their last Christmas with him. 'Often when he is lying there he will look past me to a particular point in the room with his special smile. I know he is looking at someone he loves. I am sure he is looking at Jesus'.

Nicholas died the following February.

Angus and Greg both had inoperable brain tumours and struck up a deep friendship.

Shortly before Greg died he asked his mother what heaven was like, she replied, 'Everything is golden: the people are golden, the buildings are golden and there is everything you want. For me, it will be a gold shopping mall, and I'll have a gold MasterCard.'

As he lay dying he said to his mother, 'My angel, Kelly, is here for me, but I'm not ready yet. Shut the door'

She asked what his angel looked like. He replied that she was all golden with golden hair.' As he struggled to breathe, his mother said, 'It's time for you to go with Kelly. I'll be all right.' She went to the door, opened it and called to 'Kelly'.

Greg died gently.

A short time later, as Angus was dying he struggled to get out of bed. His father held him, but Angus said, 'The golden children are running past, I want to play with them.' His father went to the door and said, 'Golden Children, Angus can't come out to play with you yet. He will come in a little while.' And so it was

After suffering with a chronic condition all his short life, Dillon had massive surgery that necessitated his being in Intensive Care, initially in a critical condition. When he was able to talk, his parents asked him each morning how he had been during the night. Each time he told them that 'the birds' had kept him awake.

As the IC unit was near a bush-bordered creek, they thought he could hear bird sounds early in the morning.

Eventually he returned home and one day was in a shopping centre. Whilst their mother did some shopping, he and his brother waited in a bookshop. Suddenly they were beside her, with Dillon saying, 'You have to come! You have to come!' and his brother saying, 'Dillon's found his birds!'

She returned with them to the bookshop, where Dillon picked up a book about angels, and on the cover the angel was depicted with lush feathered wings.

Over the years I heard many such stories. Strangely, it was never the children who initially told me, always a parent. The child was almost disinterested. I always asked them, 'Were you frightened?'

Without fail the answer was always a simple, 'No', delivered in a 'Why would I?' tone.

I used to say, 'Angels are God's way of being with us,' and they would nod in absolute agreement, and did not need to add to that. Often they would have told their parent, 'And you never ever have to be afraid of anything.' One such message from child to parent came from a three year-old girl, in the Care-Flight helicopter bringing her and her mother to Westmead. As it was landing the child said to her mother, 'There's an angel with me, mummy, and you don't have to be frightened ever again.'

I often shared my own experiences with the parents.

'My father,' continued Vera, 'had been in a nursing home for many years with Early-Onset Alzheimer's. He had not spoken or known who we were for seven years. Three weeks before my husband, our nine-year old daughter and I were leaving to go overseas for 6 weeks he developed gangrene and was expected to die, within the time we'd be away.

I made all the arrangements for the funeral, being assured by my mother and brother that the holiday was to proceed. He did not die before we left; however the night before, I spent time with him, saying all the things I needed to tell him as I said goodbye to this frail little man, unrecognisable from the father I remembered; a sturdy, short man who shouldered his way through life.

Three nights later we were in a caravan park outside Ely, in England. I had a dream so vivid that it woke me up. The Dad of my memory was standing with broad shoulders, wearing his clerical collar and a smile that lit up his face. Behind him was the minister I had arranged to conduct his funeral.

I was still half asleep and reached out to see the time, but didn't actually think through what had happened.

Next morning my husband had gone over to the ablutions block and our daughter climbed up into the bed with me, snuggling in, her little knees digging into my back. I laughed and said, 'I used to do this to Papa, I used to say, 'Me keep you warm, Daddy.'

Our daughter said, 'Me keep you warm, Mummy.' Her voice was my childhood voice, and I realised the dream was Dad coming to tell me he had died and was OK. But the gift was greater than that.

I am six years older than my brother and a rather bossy person. My brother decided early on it was better to just let me arrange things. With me not there, my brother was the one who looked after my mother and made all the necessary arrangements. It was a very special time that Dad gave them; however he made sure that I was not left out.'

I had the privilege of knowing Vera's father and mother too. They were indeed delightful people. Vera's father was a Presbyterian minister of the old school and one whom I admired. Vera's mother was a delightful, warm and caring lady and a wonderful minister's wife. (They have to be special). With parents like hers, it's no wonder Vera turned out to be the special person she is. By the way, I should cut out the word 'bossy' (above) and replace it with something else: 'firm but tactful leader' or something. Vera is great forewoman material!

The little girl who went home

Jane and her husband are friends of ours. One evening over a meal, Jane recounted an unusual story. Some years ago, she said, when she lived in another town, she suspected there was a presence in the house where they lived. She caught occasional glimpses, but never saw fully whatever it was. She thinks she must have seen just enough to suggest subconsciously that it was a small child in a nightdress.

When she and her husband were out at some evening function, her next door neighbour, Hilda, a retired school teacher, came to look after the children, who were all small at the time.

On one particular occasion, after they had been out, Hilda took Jane aside and whispered,

'Do you have a ghost in this house?'

'Why?' asked Jane.

Hilda went on to explain that after the children were put to bed, she sat at the dining room table and began to read a book. After some time she had a feeling that someone was in the next room, the kitchen. When she looked up, she could see through the doorway and was surprised to see a small child, dressed in a white nightie. She was in for an even bigger surprise. As she stared at the visitor, the child vanished. Very worried, Hilda hurried to the children's bedroom to check on her charges, but a quick look revealed that they were all there and all asleep. Besides, she knew that none of them wore a white nightdress. It was then that realisation dawned: She'd seen a ghost.

She returned to her book, a little troubled over what she had seen, but some time later, when she looked up, she saw the child again.

This time, she closed her eyes and prayed: 'Lord, take this child to where you want her to be.' When she opened her eyes, the child had again vanished.

Jane said that after that, she never had a sense of the child's presence again, and to the best of her knowledge, the child was never seen again.

This puzzling story leaves us with a question as to the identity of the little girl, but I don't think that will be known this side of eternity. Jesus had a special love of children, as the following text, and others, make plain:

People were also bringing their babies to Jesus to have him touch them. When the disciples saw this they rebuked them. But Jesus called the children to him and said, 'Let the little children come to me and do not hinder them, for the kingdom of God belongs to such as these. Luke 18:15,16. Thank you for that lovely little prayer, Hilda.

... and other true stories

Strange Lights and Other Mysteries

7

The Mystery of the Glowing Cross

No one has been able to explain adequately – scientifically or otherwise - the strange phenomenon of the glowing cross in the Lismore Cemetery, since it began to glow mysteriously one evening somewhere around the year 1918.

The occupant of the grave over which the original cross stood was a brave young man named William Steenson, who was killed while trying to stop a runaway train.

There are stories in the newspaper, the Lismore 'Northern Star,' which recorded that sometimes the cross shone so brightly, it bathed the surrounding graves in a soft light.

If one should care to Google the story, it's there for all to see, including a photo of the glowing cross which some claim may have been doctored to heighten the effect. According to a story I read, few photos are known to exist of the glowing cross, but it was so famous, there are bound to be many.

Rob, a keen photographer, was able to tell me the brand of camera as well as the lens he used to photograph the cross, both of which he still owns. The camera was a Practica with a 600mm telephoto lens. When I asked him why he used a telephoto lens he explained that the glow of the cross was more effective when photographed from a distance. He wasn't sure why the surrounding colour is red, but it was a dark night. He also gave me a photo of the cross, taken in broad daylight, which I include and which you can see is a handsome Celtic cross.

Rob and his wife Beryl remember the details surrounding the mysterious cross very clearly, when they lived there. (Beryl grew up in Lismore).

Of course there have been many suggestions as to why the cross glowed, and naturally the first one to arise was its composition. It was made of polished Balmoral granite – just like other crosses nearby which did not glow. Another theory was that its particular position may have caught the light from somewhere in Lismore, so one night, Beryl told me, all the lights in Lismore were turned off. Still the cross glowed.

Experts in various fields from stonemasons to physicists and a few in between had theories, none of which was conclusive. Perhaps the oddest – and certainly not one endorsed by any expert, was that petrified glow-worms were embedded in the granite!

As is so often the case, media exposure in the 1970s and 80s resulted in a degree of hysteria. People came to Lismore in droves to view the phenomenon. With sad predictability, the story also aroused the interest of the psychologically 'sick.' The cross was vandalised and one night in 1986 it vanished, never to be seen again.

The descendants of William Steenson were naturally upset. An anonymous donor contributed enough money to have another cross erected over the grave, made of exactly the same granite (Balmoral granite) and dimensions as the original. It has never glowed.

The original inscription on the grave however is there for all to see, which includes a quotation from a hymn written by the Anglican Bishop, Reginald Heber, Bishop of Calcutta, (1783-1826), who wrote many well-known and well-loved hymns during his brief life, for he was only 43 years of age when he died. In fact there is even a hymn tune called 'Heber': *From Greenland's icy mountain, to India's coral strand* ... etc. It's a lovely hymn; words by Heber, music by Lowell Mason.

Heber also wrote the words of the famous hymn, 'Holy Holy Holy, Lord God Almighty.'

If you ask me why I am including the above information regarding Bishop Heber, there is another little story here, a sad one, connected to our story of the glowing cross. The words on William Steenson's cross are part of a hymn that commences 'Thou art gone to the grave..'

Reginald Heber wrote it on the death of his first child.

Anyway, here is the inscription:

> Sacred to the memory of my dear husband William Thomas Thurling Steenson, who died at Lismore 30th September 1907, from injuries accidentally received in execution of his duty at Mullumbimby.
>
> Aged 29 years.

(Bishop Heber's words from the hymn follow):
Though sorrow and darkness encompass the tomb,
thy saviour has pass'd through its darkness before thee...
And the lamp of his love is thy guide through the gloom.

Those words indicate to me that William Steenson was a Christian who put his trust in the lord.

I have no idea at all why the cross glowed. For all I know, there may have been a logical explanation not yet understood, but the lamp of God's love certainly shone from the grave

There are many other Christians in Lismore and other cemeteries whose gravestones do not glow; in fact William Steenson's is the only one I've ever heard of that did glow.

I would like to complete this little story, as I have others, by reminding you that there are mysterious yet true things in this world for which we have no rational explanation, and this story is one of them.

What are the strange lights that suddenly break in on certain people's lives from time to time? If two people were looking at the same thing, would both see the same light, or would one see it and not the other? It's a philosophical question.

The theory was once put forward that the star the wise men saw on their journey to Bethlehem may have been made visible by God only to them, and no one else. No one can answer positively a question like that of course, and no one can answer the question I put regarding a light that may be visible to one and not the other at the same time.

I have sometimes wondered if my mother and Mrs Fay Bulgarie had looked up at the same time as I had seen the hand and arm in the sky, would they have seen what I saw? No one can say. Mostly, supernatural experiences seem to happen when one is alone. Ordinary, sane, rational people are suddenly confronted out of the blue by a sight or an experience that is nothing short of astonishing, to say the least.

The light that hung in the air

I would regard Jean, who contributed the two following stories as intelligent, sane and rational. I've never seen anything about her that would suggest anything else. She is a writer as well as a mother with a grown-up family. I know her well and there is nothing that would identify her as anyone different from the rest of us, yet she told me these stories that appear to have had no bearing on her life. Maybe she was just in the right place at the right time, or maybe, at some future time, she will learn why. As far as I know, the stories below are the only two times that she has had supernatural experiences. Here are her stories, in her words:

'Back in 1979, I lived in a suburb of Perth, where I found it hard to adjust to the dry, hot summer. One night I awoke at about 2:30am, feeling that I was suffocating. I got up and walked outside on the threadbare front lawn, and was immediately aware of a strange feeling coming over me. The atmosphere was weird, almost a crackling sensation, electric - the source of which revealed itself when a strange bright light appeared. It began as far to the right as I could see and continued in a straight line before me, just below the roof level of the houses opposite, then as far left as I could see. There was no traffic about and not a soul in sight. The light 'hung' there for an indeterminable space of time, then slowly faded away. Needless to say I was fairly rattled. There seemed to be no explanation for such a weird phenomenon.

Very odd, Jean. I mean, usually when a light is switched off, it simply vanishes at once. You've heard about the light at the end of the tunnel? I'm usually half-way along when someone switches it off. Yep, I know – it's an oldie. Sorry – go on…

The case of the lighted teddy bear

'This one is really strange, but true nonetheless,' said Jean, ignoring my attempt at humour. 'These days I live at Lake Macquarie, NSW, in a small studio flat – basically one room. I have a large, dark-orange teddy bear, which by day sits on my bed. At night it is moved to a lounge chair, where it is in full view from where I sleep. I awoke one morning to a strange sight. The bear was totally lit up by a bright light and was brilliant yellow. I could see its every fibre. Nothing else in the room showed any light. Then I saw the faintest, pencil-thin beam of light – I could have missed it – coming from the direction of the kitchen, a separate room with a small window. It seemed that the light had hit the bear, compounded upon itself and was somehow trapped. The beam of light disappeared, but the whole bear glowed from within. It began getting brighter and brighter, almost to brilliant white. It seemed to last quite a while, perhaps a couple of minutes. I felt quite disturbed and waited to see if the light would move sideways across the room, but it didn't. Eventually it faded within itself and my bear became its normal rusty self. I think

I will send this bear back to Kiri, my daughter, who loaned it to me for safe keeping while she travels to exotic destinations overseas.'

There's no ordinary explanation I can think of, for either of your stories, Jean. That they happened, I have no doubt. I could never imagine your making up any weird story, let alone these two. I wonder if you will ever find out? I wonder if any of us will ever find out our strange, inexplicable experiences, this side of eternity?

The Min-Min Lights

'Have you ever heard of the Min-Min lights?' I asked Janet one day.

She looked at me blankly. 'The what?'

'The Min-Min lights – you know – those mysterious lights in western Queensland. No one knows what they are. They are visible at night to travellers, and seem to follow them. Surely you've heard of them.'

The blank look remained. 'Sorry – never heard of them. Why did you ask?'

'I was just speaking to Kerry in Gunnedah on an entirely different subject. She mentioned the lights when something I said triggered a memory. She told me that some years ago, she and her husband John saw the Min-Min lights. She said she and John were driving towards Miles, in Western Queensland one night, travelling at about 100kph, when she looked out of the passenger-side window of the car and was astonished to see a ball of light keeping pace with the car. The light followed them for miles and miles. It seemed to be at ground level, she said, and rather than pass through fences, it appeared to leap over them.'

That's what the Min-Min lights are famous for – the way they seem to take an interest in human activity. People report seeing them in groups, or sometimes singly. In fact Dr Karl Shuker in his book 'The Unexplained' believes that the interest the lights appear to take in human activity suggests curiosity, rather than hostility.

To suggest they have a curios nature indicates a belief that the Min-Mins have minds, which is interesting indeed. Who could believe that the lights have minds? It seems bizarre; but who knows? Maybe something's guiding them, but the Aboriginal people knew about them.

After reading some of the bizarre theories concerning the lights that people have put forward over the years, the idea that they have thinking minds seems almost practical.

The bottom line is, no one really knows what the lights are, why they are there, or their composition. Nothing is known about them, and that's the way I like to think of them, and other things. How dull it would be, if everything on the planet and beyond was completely understood!

When I consider Your heavens, the work of Your fingers, the moon and the stars, which You have set in place, what is man, that You are mindful of him, the son of man that You care for him? Psalm 8:4,5.

... and other true stories

The matter of evil

8

Do not be afraid of those who can kill the body...
Matthew. 10:28.

Many people don't believe in evil, or evil spirits or demons, but I do. In the so-called enlightened West, those things can be explained away as psychiatric problems, chemical imbalances and so forth. Other cultures, by and large, seem more attuned to that other, darker side of human nature and supernatural beings. I counted at least seventy-eight references in the New Testament to demons, demon-possession and demoniacs. It's possible that some may be the result of a psychiatric disorder, but not all can; at least, I don't think so. St Paul speaks of the spiritual forces of evil in the heavenly realms... *therefore, put on the whole armour of God...* Ephesians 6:12,13ff .

Of course apart from scripture, people in our 21st century Western culture experience evil, or at the very least, sense it. Have you, for instance, ever walked into a room, or a house, or some other place, and felt distinctly uncomfortable – nervous, or even frightened?

Most of us have had that experience, or a similar one. Even many who claim that they don't believe in ghosties, ghoulies or anything else remotely connected to whatever goes bump in the night, have had that sort of sense of the presence of the unknown. I believe it's part of our human nature, built into us all, to recognise that there is an unseen world around us, even if consciously we deny its existence.

As I have explained before, I am not offering explanations regarding most of the incidents I'm relating, because I don't understand them myself. They are a record of what I believe are supernatural or paranormal events that occurred in my life, and other people's lives, which you can explain any way you want, believe or disbelieve. God alone knows the full story.

Because I believe in the Judaeo/Christian accounts of heaven and hell, good and evil, as contained in the Holy Bible, I believe in heaven and hell, good and evil. As I read the scriptures, I think back on one or two incidents in my own life and listen to what others have told me concerning incidents in their lives, I can say also that I believe there are evil spirits, and most religions speak of them too.

I am fortunate that I have had only one experience of an evil spirit that really frightened me, apart from the one mentioned in chapter one, which terrified many of our family members over the years – but whatever that was, it was a wooz, compared to an experience I had when I was about sixteen years of age, which was an attack, not on me physically, but I believe on my soul.

I wish I could say that I was wide awake when it happened, but it happened during sleep, or a sort of sleep. Others who have experienced a supernatural event when neither awake nor asleep, but in some twilight place, will know what I am talking about. It is not an ordinary dream experience. Of course God uses dreams to convey visions. Genesis 28:10-17 is a good example. It's the story of Jacob's ladder, (or stairway, NIV). I don't want to delve deliberately into those things. My old Scottish grandmother, a devout Calvinist Presbyterian, used to say to us, as she waggled a warning finger under our young noses (she herself was only wee): 'Dinnae ever try tae lift the veil that separates the living from the dead!' I keep repeating that, in the hope that you can discourage anyone you know who may want to go there. The dear old lady had quite an effect on my young life. Maybe it won't hurt to keep reminding you of her warning to us, her grandchildren.

I've never been tempted to do anything to lift the veil... not that I had any idea how to, of course. Dear old Granny Mitchell was a wonderful person who seemed so dour in many ways, but I can still recall her chasing my brother Peter and me around the house, wiggling her fingers, giggling, with her false teeth poking out! We'd run around the house, squealing our heads off, but it was all a great deal of fun, and we loved her.

Anyway, I'd gone to bed that night at my usual time, but some time during the night, whatever it was, came to visit me. I can see it to this day – that face, and the rest of the apparition, down to about the waist. From what I can recall of the clothes I could see they appeared to be the sort of clothing that I would recognise from pictures and so on, of a 19th century cut. If you have ever seen a movie in which there is a card-sharp dandy on Mississippi River paddle steamer, its clothing was like that.

It had blondish hair, was about middle-aged and had a yellow moustache. I think the moustache was cigar-stained because a horrible, pungent smell of cigar-smoke hung around this apparition as well as an aura of utter evil. In fact it emanated evil. It kept repeating to me, over and over, 'Let me in! Let me in!'

Something in me (it seemed to be coming from my chest somewhere) was saying vehemently 'No! No! No!' I could say nothing. Finally it vanished and I went back to normal sleep. What I can recall well is my terror. When I awoke in the morning, the smell of cigar smoke was so powerful in my nostrils that I felt physically sick. It would be a couple of years before I could stand the smell of a cigar near me.

When I recall that one-off incident in my life, I recall Jesus' words: 'Do not be afraid of those who can kill the body but cannot kill the soul. Rather, be afraid of the one who can destroy both soul and body in hell. Matthew 10:28. That 'thing' whatever it was, was one of those, I think, capable of destroying the soul, or taking it over.

Again, make of this strange story what you will. If you think I am certifiable, well and good, but so far I have managed to avoid the gents in the white coats. There are people who hear of, or read, stories like that one, and believe it's either the product of an over-fertile imagination, deliberate deceit, or evidence of lunacy. Even Christians – some of whom are friends and/or relations, refuse to accept the sorts of stories you are reading here because they are outside their own life-experiences.

...and other true stories

Let's remember that Jesus was accused from time to time of being crazy, or being in league with Beelzebub, the prince of demons. (See Luke 11:14ff).

The world is teeming with stories from ordinary folk who may have had only one supernatural/paranormal experience but are prepared to share it. Others seem to be more susceptible to the supernatural world's intrusion into their lives.

The Ouija Board

My wife Janet (pictured, aged 19) completed her High School Leaving Certificate at Gunnedah High School (NSW) at age seventeen and then went off to train as a nurse at Royal Newcastle Hospital (NSW). She said that half the girls in her final year at school decided on teaching careers, another half went nursing, while yet another half took on business careers. Maybe the rest became mathematicians and left the country. (Ness being droll again...)

In those days trainee nurses were very highly regimented, and discipline was strict. All the nurses had to 'live in' at the nurses' quarters for the four years of their training. To get married was to be removed immediately from training. Passes for evenings out were issued, but the nurses' home doors were locked at 10.30pm. (It is hard to imagine young women submitting to that sort of discipline these days). Nurses wore stiff, starched aprons and nurses' caps. Nurses in their final two years of training wore a distinctive 'bow' to the left of the face. Nursing sisters wore veils. Nurses looked like nurses. Nursing sisters looked like nursing sisters – not that they're called by that title any more. If you ever watched the TV show 'The Royal,' (or any film featuring nurses of bygone years), you will have some understanding of what it was like, for that was Janet's era as a nurse in training.

Janet's class bonded well, and to this day she maintains friendships with nurses who graduated with her.

One afternoon in the nurses' home, with an afternoon off duty and nowhere to go, some of the nurses decided to make a Ouija board and try it out. Finally it was made, a glass was fetched, and nurses were invited to place a finger on the glass and ask questions. One of those who unwisely placed a finger on the glass was Janet. Questions were asked and the glass began to move around the letters on the board. Later, Janet said that no one was controlling it. Whatever was controlling the glass appeared to become increasingly agitated at some of the questions being asked. Its movements around the board became faster, more irrational and jerky - then suddenly the glass flicked from beneath their fingers and smashed itself against the wall. Janet was petrified. Probably the others were too. She, as a young Christian, had been confronted by evil. It was the last time she ever did anything like that. Later, when she told me the story, my old Granny's warning came back to me: 'Dinnae ever try tae lift the veil that separates the living from the dead.' It has always stayed with me – and now with Janet.

A Ouija Board story from Scotland

Mac, a friend of mine, trained as a draftsman in Scotland. One day he told me an interesting story of a time he and some of his fellow trainees decided, during a quieter time and some idle discussion, to make a Ouija board. The five or six of them found a piece of suitable board, wrote out the letters and stuck them on, then found something to serve as the pointer. They all placed a finger on the pointer and began to question it. After a time the pointer began to move under their fingers. They asked it various questions, which it appeared to answer, moving from letter to letter, before someone asked, 'What is the name of the horse that will win the English Derby?' The great national horse race was to be run the following day. Obligingly, the pointer moved to various letters, which turned out to be the name of a horse in the race. Mac said he didn't know the name of any horse in the race, so when the name the board gave turned out to be the name of horse that was to run, they were all astonished. Sure enough, the following day, the horse the Ouija board had prophesied to win, did win. The effect on the boys of the win would have surprised many. Most would have been delighted – a dream come true! A sure-fire means of having foreknowledge of the winners a day or so before the race is run! Here was a recipe for untold wealth.

The boys, however, were affected differently. They became apprehensive. They were all young Christians; regular church-attenders and members of either the Boys' Brigade or Boy Scouts.

To the best of Mac's knowledge, not one of them had anything ever again to do with Ouija boards. Mac has maintained his faith, works hard for his church and is a church elder and its session clerk.

I am so glad Mac shared that story with me. Let it be a warning. I think Ouija boards are satanic. Satan never gives anything for nothing. I wonder what his 'quid pro quo' would have been, had any decided on a life of riches, courtesy of Satan? In time, probably their souls would have been required of them, when they became enslaved to him. Our life on earth is brief enough, whether we be rich or poor, while on the other side is eternity, with another choice before us: heaven or hell. Jesus had a lot to say about it. *If your hand or your foot causes you to sin, cut it off and throw it away. It is better for you to enter life maimed or crippled than to have two hands or feet and be thrown into eternal fire.* Matthew 18:8.

His reply to the devil, who promised Him all the kingdoms of the earth if He, Jesus, would worship him, says it all: *It is written, 'Worship the Lord your God and serve Him only.* Luke 4:8.

Tarot Cards

I know nothing about tarot cards. I do know that people claim to be able to read them and foretell the future and do other things, which seems to me to be hocus-pocus; a comment that will probably annoy any tarot card fans who are reading this.

Years passed after Janet's unfortunate experience with the Ouija board. By the time I heard about tarot cards in any detail I was a chaplain in the Regular Army and posted as Senior Chaplain 5th Military District. (5MD = WA. I believe the name 5th Military District has reverted to the old title: Western Command, but that happened after my time there).

In those days the three services; Navy, Army, Air Force, each had one full-time chaplain in WA who looked after their own part-time (Reserve) chaplains, who were usually parish ministers and priests.

The Army Reserve chaplains I had were great fellows from the various denominations and we had some marvellous times together.

One day I had a phone call from a soldier's wife. She had a problem, she said, and asked if I would drop out to see her, which I did later that day.

She had a most intriguing story. She told me that she, her husband and their children had been in their Army married quarter only a short time, but she knew something was terribly wrong with it. It was haunted, she told me. That set me back on my haunches a little, for it was not the sort of house one would normally associate as a choice of your average spook; at least that was my thought then. It was simply a rather old, innocuous, smallish married quarter of the type the Defence Force was gradually replacing with better housing.

The lady of the house was quite obviously distressed and nervous and said she would understand if I thought she was mad. Then she told me the story. There were regular knockings on the walls, she told me, when no one was near them, and sometimes, when they awoke in the morning, the children's clothes that had been put away carefully in drawers the previous night were scattered all over the floor. At first, she said, she and her husband thought they were scattered randomly, but on closer inspection they noted that the clothes were all exactly the same distance apart. Then, she said (and this is what prompted her to ring me), she had opened the fridge door to get something out when an unseen hand grabbed her arm. She was the only one in the house, and she screamed...

When I checked with the husband, he verified what his wife had told me but wanted none of the information to go outside in case it affected his career, for his role in the Army was highly sensitive. Suggestions of a possibly delusional soldier and wife would not help his career prospects, although it was quite obvious to me there was nothing wrong with this couple. They were well-adjusted, sensible and caring parents.

Some discreet queries on my part established some interesting news. Two tenant families in the house previously had been into tarot cards in a big way. They had left, and the next family had stayed only a couple of months before leaving for another married quarter. They'd told someone that the house they'd just left was haunted. It seemed that the tarot cards could be the problem.

I had a quiet and confidential word with my brother chaplains and it was decided to hold an exorcism, using one of the Roman Catholic or Anglican liturgies. The Presbyterian Church has no exorcism liturgy.

I forget which one we used, and didn't record it, but at the appointed time we chaplains assembled at the house. The chaplain we appointed for the task led the exorcism ritual, and after it was over, we left.

I waited for a couple of days before contacting the soldier's wife – and was relieved to learn there had been no more supernatural activity since the exorcism.

Among the chaplains there was a little celebration...

About two years later I was posted back to Oakey, Queensland, following a dreadful tragedy there, and amazingly, about a year after that, an almost identical problem surfaced at an Army married quarter near Toowoomba. The soldier and his wife told me of terrifying visitations of spirit-like things in the night, and again a quiet investigation revealed the previous family had been avid users of tarot cards.

After the previous success, I had a word with Jack, the Catholic Army Reserve chaplain at the Base and the two of us did the same thing again, with the same gratifying results.

For all I know, the link between the two strange paranormal incidents involving tarot cards could be entirely coincidental... maybe. As I said, I don't know anything about tarot cards and I don't want to. As a general rule, I also don't believe in coincidences. My story ends with the success of the two exorcisms, and apart from the two families that lived in peace with no further visitations, I don't want to know. I simply remember my grandmother's exhortation concerning the living and the dead: never attempt to lift the veil. It's sound advice. I pass it on to you (again).

Addendum: You may recall that a short time ago I mentioned that the evil apparition that visited me had a dreadful smell about it, which I associated with stale cigar smoke.

Read, however, of similar experiences other people have had and you will note many cases where evil apparitions are accompanied by a bad smell. In the Presbyterian Church in Australia we do not ordinarily use incense. Sometimes, when I have been, perhaps, to a very special service, I have caught just a tantalising whiff of incense, despite the fact that none has been at the service. It's happened only very rarely. On more than one occasion when I walked into an empty St Andrew's Church in Raglan Street Manly NSW during my time as minister there, I would catch momentarily that same elusive fragrance. It never happened in any other church. I have wondered sometimes just why. I do know that St Andrew's Manly has a very lovely aura of peace and serenity about it.

Some Animal Stories

9

Do animals save souls?

He prayeth best who loveth best
All things, both great and small;
For the dear God Who loveth us,
He made and loveth all.

From *The Rime of the Ancient Mariner* by Samuel Taylor Coleridge

Many of us are fascinated by the creatures, 'both great and small' that share our planet, and the more we understand about them, the more our fascination grows. The great 17th century English poet William Blake wrote a graphic poem (it's always been one of my favourites. I'll recite it afterwards, if you like) that reveals his fascination for tigers, and that's the name of his poem: 'The Tiger' which commences:

Tiger, tiger, burning bright
In the forests of the night;
What immortal hand or eye
Could frame thy fearful symmetry?

It's a rhetorical question. William Blake knew well Who framed the tiger's 'fearful symmetry,' for it was God. The poet reveals his faith in the beautiful words of another poem he wrote that commences,

And did those feet in ancient time
Walk upon England's mountains green;
And was the holy Lamb of God
In England's pleasant pastures seen?

That poem has been put to the moving tune *Jerusalem*, by Charles H.H. Parry.

After that little introduction, I think it reasonable to suggest that for many of us, losing a pet we love is very much akin to losing a dear human friend or family member; in fact many of us see them as part of our close family. In a special way they have become part of our lives. We love their trust, their faithfulness, their love, and the special little ways they often reserve only for us, their human family. We are their world. The wrench of parting with them through death is heart-breaking. Probably it's always been the way, but over the years we've been conditioned to believe that at the end of their lives, that's it. For them, there is nothing beyond – or so some say.

For centuries, mankind believed that birds and animals had no real intelligence. They could be taught certain things, true, but the general belief was that their behaviour was largely instinctive.

Gradually, scientists and others have begun to realise that birds, animals and even insects have minds that reason. How many of us realise that sheep are intelligent? They have a reputation for being the very opposite. Richard Gray (*Sydney Morning Herald* 21.2.2011) reports on a series of tests carried out by professor Jenny Morton, a neuroscientist at the University of Cambridge, during which it was discovered that sheep have the brainpower to equal that of monkeys and in some tests, even humans. They have advanced learning capabilities, are adaptable, can map out their surroundings and may even be able to plan ahead. The research in detail was published in the journal *Public Library of Science One*. (Think about that when you tuck into your next lamb chop).

Yes, I'm a vegetarian. While acknowledging the right of people to eat what they like (Mark 7:17-19), whenever I see a steak or a chop, all I really see are terror and blood, suffering and death, although I freely admit that at one time as a keen young carnivore I could tear into a steak or chop with the best of them.

When I was a boy we had a house cow; a Jersey called Sally, who was amazingly intelligent. By a mysterious means she would open the farm gate, hit the road, find another open farm gate, enter, and help herself to whatever she liked in garden and/or crop. We boys were forever being accused of leaving the farm gate open. One day however, my father caught Sally in the act. She must have watched how the chain was dropped over a peg set in the gatepost, and soon worked out how to nudge the chain off the peg with her nose.

Clever girl!

Some time ago there was a thought-provoking little article in 'The Newcastle Herald,' written by John von Radowitz which was headed 'Flies Make Up Their Minds To Be Irritating.' The article went on to record that scientists have found evidence of free-will in fruit flies!

The article said that if confirmed, the discovery might overturn basic assumptions about differences between humans and animals. Some researchers, the article continued, are asserting that the blowfly or wasp that will not leave you alone is not innocently reacting to a biological program, but is actually *choosing* to be a pest!

Dr George Sugihara, a researcher from the Scripps Institution of Oceanography at the University of California wrote, 'The results indicate a mechanism which might be common to many other animals and could form the biological foundation for what we experience as free will.'

It's fine to ponder the intelligence of birds, animals, fish and even insects, but there must be more, so let's move on. It would be rather boring if all we could say about the other creatures that share our world is that they have intelligence. Even computers have intelligence!

While we may not be sure about insects, we do know that animals have personality. Not only do we know it from our experience with our own pets, but again science is reaching out. There have been numerous studies done on animals in the wild to confirm it. There was quite a famous study on kangaroos some time ago, when a mob of kangaroos was studied. All were given names and their habits and activities watched and recorded carefully. It was soon unmistakably clear that each animal had a distinct personality. The results were brought to us via a fascinating TV program. Other studies, such as the fascinating TV documentary, *Meerkat Manor* confirm it. It would seem all animals and birds have personalities that identify them individually.

Intelligence and personality are great, and some believe that the animal kingdom is confined to those alone; but perhaps there's more.

To ponder the possibility that animals may have a soul is to move into largely uncharted territory.

Many of the world's hundreds of religions believe animals have a soul. The religion with which most of us in Australia are familiar with, or have heard about, is Judaeo/Christian. Let's take that as our basis, and turn to the Judaeo/Christian account of earth's beginnings, found in the ancient Book of Genesis, the first book in the Bible.

The biblical evidence that animals have a soul is there, although a little knowledge of the original language is a help.

It all hinges on the Hebrew word *Nephesh*, translated in English as 'breath of life,' but which in Hebrew means 'soul.'

First, according to the Book of Genesis, (chapter 1, verse 22) God blessed the animals.

Dr John H. Sailhamer, writing in 'The Expositor's Bible Commentary' says: 'The importance of the blessing in Genesis chapter 1, verse 28, cannot be overlooked: ... the living creatures have already been blessed on the fifth day (verse 22); thus the author's view of the blessing extends beyond man to the whole of God's living creatures.'

An American writer, Kit Goodwin, points out that in the Jewish Bible 'soul' is mentioned 244 times. In those 244 cases, there are only four where a word other than 'nephesh' is used to describe 'soul'. Very significantly for our case, Genesis 1:30 has these words: *...and to all the beasts of the earth and all the birds of the air and all the creatures that move on the ground – everything that has the breath of life* (nephesh combined with chayyah means every living creature has a soul), *I give every green plant for food. And it was so.*

That suggests to me that in the beginning, no animal was carnivorous, and that suggestion is confirmed in the Book of Isaiah chapter 11.

When we turn to the Old Testament and to the Book of Numbers, chapter 22:20ff, we find the story of Balaam and his donkey. Balaam, a non-Israelite prophet, was proving something of a problem for God, in that he was trying to please both God and Balak, the Moabite king. Against God's wish, Balaam was on his way to meet Balak, who wanted Balaam to put a curse on the Israelites, who were preparing to advance across the Jordan, when God put an angel with a drawn sword on the road before him. The donkey saw the angel and shied away. Balaam severely beat her for turning away, for he could not see the angel. Twice more the same thing happened and twice more Balaam beat the donkey with his staff. Then God allowed the donkey to speak, then spoke to Balaam through the donkey, before opening the prophet's eyes so that he could see the angel with the drawn sword. *The angel of the Lord asked him, 'Why have you beaten your donkey these three times? I have come here to oppose you because your path is a reckless one before me. The donkey saw me and turned away from me these three times. If she had not turned away I would certainly have killed you by now, but I would have spared her.'* Numbers 22:32,33. You'll find the whole story in Numbers 22. Make of this story what you will, but the bottom line is that God gave pre-eminence to the donkey, allowing her to speak with a human voice. He also said that he would have killed Balaam, but spared the donkey, if Balaam had continued not to listen. The story supports other Biblical evidence of the special place God has for animals. He gave them a soul and uses all His creatures for His purposes.

Moving on again, I've had animals all my life and have loved them all, as I am certain you've loved each of yours. Those in close and loving contact with their animals see in them what humanity accepts as the highest, noblest qualities: patience, devotion, forgiveness, love, loyalty, trust. Some write off those virtues simply as anthropomorphisms – that is, bestowing human qualities on animals, but we who love animals and who are loved in return, may well scoff at such a simplistic view. The anecdotal evidence to the contrary is universal.

The animals that share our lives offer a love that is selfless, and a faithfulness that is boundless. All they want in return is our love and faithfulness. Nothing soul-less could possess those qualities. They deserve our love and protection. People who are wantonly cruel to the helpless are capable of any atrocity, to my mind.

There are countless tales of faith and love in the animal kingdom, but one in particular that touches hearts is the true story of 'Greyfriars Bobby.'

Bobby was a Skye terrier, and his owner was an Edinburgh policeman by the name of John Gray. The constable patrolled the Edinburgh streets, usually at night, back in the mid-nineteenth century, and was accompanied always by his lovely little Skye terrier, Bobby.

Unfortunately, in 1858 John Gray fell ill and died. Among those at his funeral at Greyfriars Kirkyard in Edinburgh was his little mate, Bobby.

That night, John Gray's relatives discussed what to do with Bobby, but the little dog had made up his own mind. During the night he slipped his lead and ran back to the cemetery.

The following morning the curator of the cemetery found him lying on his master's grave and shooed him home. The next morning however, there was Bobby back again, defiantly lying on his master's grave and was again sent off. The same thing happened again and then again.

The graveyard curator, a kind man, took pity on the grieving little animal, lying there in the cold, and brought him some food. That was the start of an amazing saga of faithfulness.

Bobby was there every day, for the rest of his life. Fourteen years later, in 1872, he died.

The beautiful little dog was buried not far from his master.

The story inspired the people of Edinburgh and beyond. A statue of Bobby was erected in Edinburgh, and many visitors to the city go especially to see it, and to wonder at such devotion, which without doubt stands at the very pinnacle of love and faithfulness.

The story of Bobby is not unique; nor are the stories confined to dogs. There are countless tales of animals of all sorts, as well as birds, which have displayed intelligence, as well as acts of peerless love, faith, devotion and loyalty in their interaction with us. We know they can fret when we are away from them. We know they can grieve when we die – I'm sure it's the same grief we feel when they die.

Here's a very beautiful and true story, which takes us to Africa in 2012. In March of that year Lawrence Anthony, who was known as 'the elephant whisperer,' died of a heart attack, aged 61. In fact that is the title of a book he wrote in conjunction with Graham Spence. (We bought our copy on Kindle, but it's available as a hard copy from Amazon). The book is a powerful read and I can recommend it. Lawrence Anthony devoted his life to elephants and their welfare. Stories are legion of his saving elephants, and of the amazing way they responded to him.

Working from a reserve he established called Thula Thula in Zululand, Anthony concentrated his work on the rehabilitation of traumatised elephants, with amazing results. It seems that, just as horse whisperers have a mysterious way of communicating with horses which instinctively trust them, elephants understood and trusted Lawrence Anthony. His death was sudden and unexpected. Two days later, a herd of twenty elephants from the Thula Thula reserve arrived at the Anthony home. They had travelled about twenty kilometres. Soon after, another herd of about eleven elephants arrived. This amazing, wonderful story is confirmed by Mrs Francoise Anthony and their two sons. Mrs Anthony believes that the elephants seemed to know that her husband had died, and she believes had come to grieve and pay their respects. It seems completely plausible to me. Why else would they have come, when they hadn't been to the house for over a year? To suggest it was some strange coincidence borders on the incredible. The mysterious connection between humans and the animals we love is hard to deny in the face of this story, and other stories. Nephesh chayyah: 'a soul in every creature,' and our souls are interconnected in a way we cannot understand, but God does, for He created us all.

Mrs Anthony said the elephants stayed for two days and two nights and left on the morning of the third day, to return to their grazing lands.

Rob Kirby of Beliefnet wrote of Anthony's death: Planet earth lost a passionate advocate for those who cannot speak for themselves this past March. But the most extraordinary aspect of this story is how a herd of wild elephants in a game reserve in South Africa paid their respects to the death of their man-friend and protector, Lawrence Anthony.

Let us all say 'Amen' to that.

The greatest love is the love that gives up one's own life for another, and there are documented cases where that peerless, self-sacrificial love has been observed in the animal kingdom.

One case, recorded in 'National Geographic' some years ago occurred in Yellowstone National Park in the USA. After a devastating forest fire, rangers were sent in to assess the damage. One man found a bird that had been charred to little more than ashes, which he found at the foot of a tree. When he moved the bird with his stick he was astonished to see three small chicks, very much alive, scurry from under the wings of their dead mother. It can be surmised that as the fire approached, the mother bird gathered her little brood under her wings.

As the fire scorched her little body, she resisted the temptation to fly, preferring to die so that her little ones would live.

To add credence to that story, the late Mrs Rae Fraser, wife of the late Rev Bruce Fraser, has a similar account of an incident in Victoria

... and other true stories

(Australia). Rae was one of God's special saints. We knew her and Bruce during our time in Western Australia, where they also lived at that time. As a brief aside, years ago, Rae was diagnosed with bowel cancer, and many people around the country and indeed the world, prayed for her recovery. There was no mistaking the cancer: the doctors confirmed it with a biopsy. When they opened her up to remove the cancer however, there was nothing to excise – not even scar tissue. The doctors were amazed. One refused to call it a miracle. 'We call that spontaneous regression,' he told her. Another doctor, a Christian, smiled. 'Rae,' he said, 'there's no other word for it – the complete disappearance of your tumour is a miracle!' Rae lived many more years to cast her lovely Christian radiance on the world.

Anyway, aside over, she wrote a small devotional booklet, called *Thru Trials to Peace*. We treasure our copy. The book contains fifty-two devotions. Devotion number twenty-one is called 'A Refuge Prepared for Us.' She uses a text from Psalm 61:4b: *Let me take refuge in the shelter of Your wings*. In the story that follows, Rae describes the horror of a massive bushfire close to the home where she and Bruce lived in country Victoria, and how her husband went out to fight the fire with the volunteers. Many homes were destroyed as well as a beautiful little historic Anglican Church not far from them. Rae writes, 'We decided to go out to see for ourselves, and as I walked up the path I was tearful, seeing wisps of smoke from piles of wood on the ground. Nothing had been saved! I kicked an old, feather-filled altar cushion that was smoking on the path, and to my amazement, as it turned sideways with my push, out ran four little yellow chicks... It had not been a cushion, but a mother hen, which died sheltering her babies under her wings!' Rae and the others took the rescued chicks to a nearby farmhouse. Wild bird and domestic hen, each was prepared to sacrifice herself for her little ones. Love so deep is the greatest of spiritual virtues, transcending intelligence and personality, pointing to *nephesh chayyah* – a soul in every creature. The ancients must have known that sort of love existed in the animal kingdom, and identified it with the love of God, for another of the Psalms expresses that love in the following words: *He will cover you with His feathers, and under His wings you will find refuge.* (Psalm 91, verse 4).

In Judaeo/Christian writings, the lamb is depicted as the symbol of innocence and purity; the perfect sacrifice. The scriptures contain, for instance, the story of a poor man's beloved lamb that drank from his cup and slept in his arms (2 Samuel 12:1-13) while the Book of Revelation – that strange, mysterious book of apocalyptic writings, tells of *the Lamb in the midst of the throne ... who will guide them to springs of living water.* (Rev.7:16). Of course for Christians the lamb symbolises the Lamb of God, Jesus Christ, God's Son.

Can we push the boundaries even further? What's the possibility of our loved animals being with us in heaven – if we believe in heaven, that is, and I certainly do. For those who have lost a loved animal friend through death, the thought of being reunited forever is a joyous thought. I long to see all those I've 'loved and lost awhile' and it's my earnest prayer that I will do so. I believe I will.

Mark Twain, the famous author of such great works as 'Tom Sawyer' and 'Huckleberry Finn' certainly believed in heaven, and his prayer was that his loved animals would have a place there too. He was a lover of cats and wrote:

Heaven will not heaven be,
If my cats aren't there with me.

The journey from here on is rather one of faith and hope – together with love, of course. Let's look at a great biblical prophecy of the end times, when the whole earth will be redeemed, and it has a lot to do with animals:
The wolf shall live with the lamb,
The leopard shall lie down with the goat,
The calf and the lion and the yearling together,
And a little child will lead them.
The cow will feed with the bear;

Their young shall lie down together;
And the lion shall eat straw like the ox.
The infant will play near the hole of the cobra,
And the young child put his hand into the viper's nest.
They will neither harm nor destroy on all My holy mountain,
And the earth shall be full of the knowledge of the Lord
As the waters cover the sea. Isaiah 11: 6-9.

In the New Testament, we find three references to heaven using the word 'paradise' which was originally a Persian word, meaning literally, a 'walled garden.' It is sometimes used to describe the Garden of Eden. The Jewish people believe heaven is 'the new Eden,' when creation is returned to the way God intended it to be.

Conjecture takes over here, but it's hard to imagine a garden in which there are no birds or animals. Quite apart from conjecture, there is hope, and faith, and there is also trust that God, Who loves us as we can never love, will never destroy our love, for as Paul wrote, 'Love never fails.'

I don't like to talk about our children, lest you consider it boasting, so forgive me if I tell you about Tonkie, our Tonkinese cat. He has us trained into his routine, and he and Jock our Border Collie get on famously together... On the understanding, of course, that Tonkie is boss, for after all, he is a cat!

Tonkie and I have a morning routine: I arise. So does Tonkie. I go downstairs. So does Tonkie (usually resting his six kilo frame comfortably across my shoulders). I prepare Tonkie's early light brekkie before returning upstairs. So does Tonkie, after his breakfast. I have a shower. Tonkie does NOT join me, but later, as I brush and comb my hair, he is waiting to have his fur brushed and his face combed too. I have a shave. So does Tonkie... at least, he *thinks* he is having a shave. He jumps up on the bathroom cabinet, waiting for me to finish my shave, using an electric razor (a Remington with the three cutters). While he is not looking, I remove the top that houses the cutting blades, revealing the three revolving arms underneath that drive them, so Tonkie really has a facial massage followed by a body massage. He's the only cat I've ever known that doesn't mind an electric thing buzzing noisily around his face – in fact he enjoys it! He is so funny.

That's the morning routine, but he lets me know when he is requiring some quality time during the day. If he is feeling in need of some extra affection, he'll wander into the study while I'm working on the computer, jump on the desk and utter a single miaow. If he thinks I am not responding quickly enough, his next ploy is to head-butt my mouse-hand, usually at some critical point when I have a whole paragraph highlighted. The mouse almost invariably seems to fly up to DELETE on the menu bar, and at once the paragraph disappears before my eyes. Irritation melts when those gorgeous, calm blue eyes meet my small green irritated ones, and I dissolve into laughter. He also enjoys head-butting my hand when I'm using a pen to gain my attention, which is a display of affection. Many of my hand-written documents contain unexpected squiggles and dramatic lines running through them, as if the writer was operating his pen while sitting on the back of a flat-bed truck being driven along a corrugated road at great speed. If ever you receive something hand-written by me that looks like that, or a printed document with great chunks missing, you'll know who has been demanding my immediate and undivided attention – and why? The answer is the special bond based on love, and when one thinks about it, Tonkie's priorities are right. I recognise it each time I pick him up and hear his little purring machine rumble into life. I'm also reminded of it every time I hear that plaintive miaow at my feet, and looking down, see Tonkie, looking up, wanting to be picked up and nursed, and given a cuddle or two. That's love. Animals can teach us the right priorities in life. Jock the Border Collie is the same, and I am reminded of his love each time those gentle brown eyes look up at me without a trace of duplicity, and each time he runs to greet us, his face alight with joy. He hates to be away from us and consequently we hate not to have him with us, wherever we go.

At one time, a mysterious, fatal illness began to afflict certain children in 19th century Britain (and possibly elsewhere). No one knew what it was, so they called it 'Marasmus' from a Greek word, meaning 'to wither' or perhaps 'to decay.' Marasmus is a disease that still afflicts poverty-stricken people in various places such as India, but its cause, I seem to recall, is the decay of chronic malnutrition, whereas the British children had plenty of good food and everything needed to sustain healthy life. The fact is, the children simply withered away and died, when they shouldn't have. They were all orphaned and/or abandoned babies who were put in orphanages and raised in clinically perfect conditions. They should have thrived, but instead they died, while children raised in dirt and squalor at home, thrived. Why? That was indeed a puzzle. It should have been the other way around, the experts thought. Finally, the reason was discovered and the solution applied. Soon, the children in the orphanages began to thrive. The answer was really so simple. The authorities realised at last that where children were shown love and care, they blossomed as they should have. Children raised clinically, fed and watered by the book and picked up only to be attended to, died. The missing ingredient, so vital to life itself, was love, affectionate touching, hugging, the sound of a loving voice. Someone experimented – with great success. From then on, the nursing staff who had been discouraged from doing so before, were encouraged to pick up and cuddle the children and show them the love they needed in order to live. Marasmus in the orphanages disappeared, never to be seen again.

Some time later, an experiment on baby rats was conducted, with exactly the same results. Nearly all the baby rats taken from the mother and given all the clinical requirements for life, but nothing else, died. The survivors were stunted physically and emotionally immature. Life's vital force is love, and it applies to all living creatures.

When I feed the topknot pigeons each morning, that gather on our back lawn, I watch the little family of about six as they run around my feet, industriously pecking up the seed, trusting me not to harm them. I love their innocent trust. Rev Ray, a knowledgeable friend told me recently that the correct name for the topknot pigeon is the crested pigeon.

Recently at a Police Chaplains' seminar, Fr Paul, a fellow police chaplain, told me of the magpies he fed each morning at a former parish. During spring, when magpies are at their most difficult and irritable, they regularly attacked the children at the Catholic school. Fr Paul thought it wrong to hurt the magpies in any way, for the birds thought they were protecting their young, so he and the children commenced feeding them raw mince, and very soon the magpies realised that Fr Paul and the children were their friends. One day, Fr Paul told me, as he stood on the verandah of his home, a mother magpie stood at the bottom of the verandah steps and called to him persistently, peering up at him with her beady little black eyes as only magpies can do. He was puzzled, unable to work out what she wanted of him. Finally, exasperated by his obtuseness, she marched up the steps to where he stood, took the cuff of his trousers in her beak, and 'pulled' him down the steps. He was amazed to discover that she was leading him to her chicks, to introduce him to them!

There was another occasion, he said, on a blistering hot day the mother magpie shepherded her little chicks to him. Already they were close to suffering heat exhaustion and possible death.

He put out bowls of ice water for them, which they loved and it doubtlessly saved their lives.

The mother magpie, a wild bird, trusted him to save her babies.

Don't tell me animals and birds don't have a soul! Look closer at that little one who loves and trusts you, who shares your life, who is beside you in joy and sorrow, who can comfort you simply by being with you. Once, when I was grieving the loss of some loved person, Bonnie, our border collie at the time, knew something was wrong, recognised grief, and licked away a tear or two as she did her best to comfort me. They know when we are happy. They care when we are sad. Do you really believe that apart from a brain and a heart and other necessary organs, there is nothing else? Look again! When I look into Tonkie's eyes or Jock's eyes, I can see signs of heaven there, for I see love and trust, innocence and purity of heart.

Well-known author and television producer Jennifer Skiff has a moving new book (published by Allen and Unwin) on the shelves called 'The Divinity of Dogs.' There was a very positive review of the book in a recent edition of the Uniting Church magazine, Insights. It's a book with many contributions from dog owners who tell of the miracles of their dogs. The writer calls for strident action against cruelties to animals that are officially tolerated. If Jennifer's book doesn't touch your heart and challenge your thinking, nothing will.

If at the end of my life the Lord in His mercy and grace welcomes me into heaven, my hope is that, together with those human family and friends whose loss I've mourned over the years, I'll be greeted also by those dear and faithful, four-footed friends who shared my life on earth and who will, I pray, continue to share it through all eternity.

Now let me share some stories regarding ghostly animal sightings. Mind you, I don't connect these sightings with the souls of the animals, and in the same way I don't think 'human' ghosts are the actual souls, which have gone off to wherever God has assigned them.

A Fleeting Visit by Singh

As told by LS

'My brother and his family were the very fond owners of a beautiful Burmese cat by the name of Singh, who came into their lives well before my brother reached the age of retirement. Singh was a very loving boy, who brought nothing but laughter and sunshine into their lives. He would spend much of his time curled around my brother's shoulders, or stretched out on his lap. My brother would be typing away on his computer, when good old Singh, deciding that his Dad needed a helping hand, would leap onto the keyboard and take over, thus leaving my brother's work in a jumbled mess!

When my brother and sister in-law travelled, Singh and Bonnie their Border Collie always accompanied them. They never took a vacation without them. As the years went by, Singh got old and his health started to fade. There was a time when my brother and sister in-law were going overseas. They asked me if I would mind taking care of their beloved Singh. I was so thrilled at the very thought of having him with me for a time. He soon settled in, and was very much at home with me. I enjoyed every moment with him! Singh sat on my lap, no matter where I sat, even at my computer. As I typed away one day, he decided that I needed a helping hand, so leapt onto my keyboard, leaving behind a string of funny writing on my page. He certainly was a beautiful little fellow with his funny little ways and I loved him dearly. Sadly, not long after my brother and sister in-law returned home, Singh passed on. My brother in particular took his little friend's death very hard. As I sat at my computer some time later, totally absorbed in the work that I was doing for my Church, I became aware of a strange presence near me .I looked around, but no-one was there. Suddenly however I saw the full form of a cat emerge from out of nowhere. The first thing that came to view was a noble face, followed by a beautiful silken body. In a flash, he vanished. It was Singh; I recognised him at once. I was absolutely overjoyed by his presence. He came to show us that he hadn't really left us; he would be with us always, in spirit.'

Thank you for that lovely story, LS. I am intrigued by that line: '… I saw the full form of a cat emerge from out of nowhere.' At once I recalled the experience of the arm and the hand that appeared in the sky from out of nowhere (see 'My first supernatural experience'). You've put that very well. I describe it as like an arm emerging from between two curtains that overlap, but you've said it better. It makes me wonder if, every now and then, some 'crack' or 'break' occurs between this world and the unseen world, and we get unexpected glimpses.

Helen's Story

(As told by her)

Helen is a lady whom I know well. She is both a talented writer and a gifted artist who designed the cover of this book. Her own book is not far from being published. She has a very interesting and beautifully told story here for us – one to make us think, too.

'My mum Gwen loved birds. Well, that is to say, she had to love birds.

Each year as she aged it became more difficult to find her a gift for her birthday. She had drawers full of embroidered hankies, beautiful soaps that were never used and more nighties than she would ever need.

Her eighty-seventh birthday loomed and thoughts of 'what will I give her this year?' constantly nagged at me.

A potted plant seemed like a nice idea, so I trotted along to the nursery to pick out some instant colour. I ambled around the petunias, pelargoniums and primroses, not very excited at the choice. I was amused by the proliferation of flowers that started with P: primulas, poppies and pinks; it was becoming a game.

Then I saw my gift: Two ceramic budgies sat on the side of a ceramic birdbath. Mum already had a birdbath, which she filled habitually for the native birds. Discriminately, she always shooed the Indian mynahs away. 'Noisy, horrible birds' she would grumble. She didn't grumble at much in life.

The two budgies tickled my fancy, so I bought her a pair that gazed lovingly into each other's eyes.

They were received with a curious look and a small chortle, then Blue-Tacked to the balcony railing so that they could commune with their brethren.

They were the centre of interest for a short-lived period, but she always smiled at them when she watered the garden, as if they were in on her joke.

Others in the family loved the budgies and very soon they were joined by a cocky of indeterminate lineage and a sweet little American cardinal bird. When travelling, the family focused on bringing her back a souvenir bird from their various destinations. By the time she turned ninety-two, her balcony and garden were crammed with a multitude of varied birdlife. Domestic and exotic lived side by side, rarely, if ever quarrelling. She communed with her little friends on a firmly imaginative basis and was constantly amused and slightly embarrassed by her nickname of the 'bird lady of Carlingford'.

The end took a while to grab hold of her – she was a fighter – a strong woman. The kind we don't make so much these days. Possibly two world wars and a depression had something to do with it.

Her granddaughter, Julia, lived in Seattle so they saw each other only after long periods apart. They had a strong bond; a special bond. They thought of each other often, with a smile and a loving memory of their last visit.

Mum's death came suddenly. It crept up on us while we were expecting a longer decline. Two days and she was gone. She died at 2.15 on a sunny afternoon in August.

We were grateful. It was peaceful, and we sat in her sunny hospital room remembering childhood experiences.

At the same time in Seattle, Julia was arriving home with her two boisterous boys. When they walked into the house they were surprised to see a small bird sitting on the dining table. It sat and stared at them, and they stared back at the bird. No one spoke. No one moved. They just froze in the surreal moment. Julia walked over and picked up the bird, which was happy to sit on her hand. She took it outside where it flew off into the sunset.

The next moment her phone rang. It was a call from me, telling her that grandma had just died. The bird lady was saying her goodbye. Her messenger had flown in and left the love behind.'

A strange farewell story from Malaysia

Some years ago, while a chaplain in the Australian Army I was posted to Watsonia Barracks (I believe it is now called Simpson Barracks) Watsonia, Victoria. Among the various units I visited regularly was a RAEME (Royal Australian Electrical and Mechanical Engineers) unit under the command of a Major Frazer, who was a very fine man. After going around his troops and having a yarn or two, my final visit was to his office for another yarn or two and to check up on any problems. He'd had an interesting career and for a while he'd had a posting in Malaysia. I can't remember what he said he did there now, but as with everyone posted there, the rule was that each household had to employ an amah, or servant girl – the higher the rank, the more amahs one had to employ, for the wages were very low among the locals. The same rule applied to all the Defence Force families (who were mainly RAAF) posted to Butterworth. I don't think anyone minded, for all the amahs I heard about were wonderful young women, and many remained friends with the Australian families after they returned to Australia. Major Frazer and his wife and family had a very pleasant young lass whose name was Daisy working for them. One day Daisy's father, who lived with her, died, so she had some time off.

She had not returned to work when one night there was a phone call from Daisy: 'Major Frazer! I am so terrified! There is a strange creature in my house! Please, come at once!' Help me!' Quite alarmed, Major Frazer left immediately for Daisy's house. When he arrived, she showed him up to her room where, he said, a very large bird – he seemed to recall it was one of the owl family, or perhaps it was an owl, sat, looking at them. Daisy was terrified and kept saying something about 'my father.'

As the owl didn't appear to be in any particular hurry to depart, Major Frazer grabbed a blanket, threw it over the bird, took it to the window and let it go. He said it flew into a nearby tree and sat there in the dark, looking at them, wearing a slightly indignant expression, if you can imagine an owl with an indignant expression. Anyway, he said, it didn't appear too happy about the treatment, but accepted it.

'What sort of a creature is it?' Daisy asked him as the Major prepared to leave.

'Have you never seen one before?' he replied; 'It's an owl. They're nocturnal, usually.'

She shook her head. 'I have not seen one before – ever. All I know is that when my father was dying, he told me that he would return to me to say goodbye, in the form of a creature I have never seen before.'

The Strange Case of the Neighing Horse

I have never heard a voice from out of nowhere, let alone a horse that neighed, but a friend of mine had an interesting story.

John was a dentist in Manly and lived in that area all his life, apart from war service as a navigator on Liberator bombers in the South Pacific zone. He had one of the best minds I've ever known and was quite brilliant; especially in regard to the classics.

Quite apart from that, he was a humorous, warm and compassionate man, upon whom I could rely.

I first met John when I was called as minister to St Andrew's Presbyterian Church Manly, where John was one of the elders and the session clerk (the minister's unpaid, right-hand helper, confidante, organiser and adviser, among other roles, who also keeps the minutes of the elders' meetings. I very much valued his wisdom).

He once told me of a time when he had a patient in his chair at Manly. He started by looking at the patient's address, which was in Balgowlah.

'That's interesting,' John told the patient as he motioned to the nurse to hand him the hammer and chisel (I made up that bit about the hammer and chisel – you probably guessed that). 'The house where you live used to be a vacant block, owned by a veterinary surgeon, when I was a boy. We lived not far from it, and we kids played there. There was a friendly old horse on the block too, I recall. One day, when we were playing there, the Vet arrived and told us we'd have to leave. He was going to have to put the horse to sleep because it had something badly wrong with it, and he didn't want us to see him do it, fearing it would upset us. When we went back a day or so later, of course the horse was no longer there, and we were sad.'

'I remember the patient giving me a very strange look,' said John, 'but his reply was even stranger: 'It may be more interesting than you think,' he told me. 'It explains why my wife and I sometimes hear the sound of a neighing horse, seemingly somewhere very close by, if not in the house itself.'

'That whole street is now just wall to wall houses and units,' John said. 'There is no way a horse could possibly live anywhere near there.'

It's one of those inexplicable stories. It seems to me that sometimes, when someone dies, some part remains locked in that spot. The theory has been put that ghosts are really shades or shadows of people or animals whose spirits did not move on completely to the other side – but there am I, guessing again. Only God knows the real story.

A Mysterious Photograph

Wendy Randall

'My sisters Merle and Cookie had come over from South Africa for a holiday around about 1989 and we planned to take them on a ferry ride down the Swan River in Perth, Western Australia. We were on board the ferry and just as it pulled away from the moorings, Merle turned to photograph the Perth foreshore.

Some time later she had her photos developed (no digital cameras at that time) and saw to her amazement an image of a cat super-imposed on the corner of that photo she took of the Perth foreshore. Neither she nor the photographic shop could explain the phenomenon. I have seen the photo myself. It is not something that could possibly be explained away as a strangely-shaped cloud, an aeroplane, or anything else but a cat.'

The Day Sheiba Came Back

This is a story told to me by Robina. I've known her all her life, and I certainly know her well enough to assure you she is not given to fanciful thinking or daydreams of that nature. She is however an animal lover, and has a small business, dog-walking other people's dogs and looking after them in their homes when the owners are away.

'When I was growing up we had a family dog named Sheiba. She was a cattle dog cross and came to live with us when she was about two years old, after following my young brother home. He had stopped to pat her and they formed an instant bond. Nobody came forward to claim her so we kept her, which was a very happy arrangement for us all. Sheiba was such a beautiful, loving and loyal girl and we loved her dearly.

Several years later when I was an adult, Sheiba and our other dog Dagger, came to live at my house. Sheiba was about 14 years old by then and we had a good eighteen months together. She passed away suddenly at home one night and it was very quick and peaceful. My brother came over and we buried her in the back yard. We were all devastated and missed her greatly.

One of my family chores each morning was to let Dagger out for the day. From the back door there were about six steps leading down into the yard. I was just about to head down the steps when, to my utter amazement, I saw Sheiba standing, side on, at the bottom of the stairs. She was in full colour and as clear as day. There was no mistaking what I saw. I raced down the stairs, but before I could get to the bottom, she had vanished.

I went back inside, struggling to comprehend what I'd seen, and yet overjoyed too. I said nothing to my partner, because I felt that he might not believe me. In fact I didn't mention it to anybody for quite a while. I needed time to process in my mind my strange experience. The more I thought about it, the more I felt as though Sheiba had delivered a very special message; letting me know that she was okay and that she was still around. I felt honoured.

That happened ten years ago, but I remember it as though it were yesterday. I'll certainly never forget our lovely dog Sheiba, and the day she came back to pay me a visit.'

The ghost cat of Manly Manse

First, a pocket-history of the manse that you may never hear, outside this yarn. (Most of this comes under the *and other true stories* category of the book's title, but it's interesting. You can sleep through this if you wish).

The manse attached to St Andrew's Presbyterian Church Manly is a particularly lovely building, created in sandstone and double-storey, classified by the National Trust, for it was built circa 1890. It has a great position. Its top-storey windows and verandahs at one time had 180-degree views of the sea and Sydney harbour. I once saw a postcard of the manse, taken somewhere around the year 1900 from down near the ferry terminal. The manse residents of those days certainly would have had those lovely views. At least one can still look across Raglan Street to the park and the oval.

By the time we (the Ness family) arrived in 1995, the views were largely gone, but if we stood out on the upstairs verandah and did a spot of neck-craning, we could just make out a glimpse of sea to the east and a glimpse of harbour to the south.

I was the tenth minister called to the parish. Most, of course, are dead, but at time of writing Rev Derek Bullen is the current minister, and the two immediately before me are still alive and well: Rev Stephen de Plater who is still a minister in NSW and Rev James Reid (now into his 90's and still active and living in WA).

The minister before them is also alive and well, I believe, and went to a church in the USA, but I'm sure he's retired now too.

The only other I recall meeting, and that was many years ago, was the Rev Jack Richardson, now long dead. Jack was a delightful man who did some part-time lecturing at St Andrew's United Faculty of Theology, within Sydney University, where I was a student for the ministry. He taught us Hebrew, but was a classics scholar.

During the history of the manse, quite a few notable ministers lived there, among them one who was blind. He had a close friend – the famous Australian bush poet, A.B. ('Banjo') Paterson (1864-1941). Sometimes Banjo would visit the manse and take his blind friend for a walk along the Esplanade at Manly. Apparently Banjo enjoyed a drink or two, and sometimes arrived at the manse slightly the worse for wear. I was told that a standing joke among some of the locals of the day, when they saw the minister being guided by Banjo, said that it was a case of 'the blind leading the blind.' That story was told to me by someone who was related to the minister, and has been passed down through his family. The story I am about to tell you was also told to me by that same family member.

Look, if you are feeling a bit sleepy, I'll let you nod off for a while but, sitting here before the fire, the third cup of hot chocolate still warm in my hand, the French brass clock ticking away in the room, I am going to tell it anyway, whether you nod off or not... yes, I know we still haven't arrived at the ghost cat. I'll get there - eventually, like the end of my sermons.

I love the story I am about to tell you, for it's a story of a little romance... The blind minister had a daughter who lived with him at the manse. From what I understand, they were the only two in residence.

The daughter tended to the needs of her elderly father with true daughterly devotion, but she was attractive and in time caught the eye of a young architect who lived across the valley (somewhere up around St Patrick's). They fell in love, and he asked her father for permission to marry her, who refused. I suppose in a way we can understand his reluctance, for once she was gone, who would look after him? We must remember that many of the facilities that exist for the care of the aged these days hadn't even been thought of back then.

The daughter refused to marry without her father's blessing, but the couple were in love, so each evening she stood out on the manse verandah and waved a lantern across the valley. (There were few buildings between them in those days, and certainly no high-rises). He waited for her signal, and waved his lantern back, which was virtually their only way of staying in touch.

The story ends on a happy note, for eventually the girl's father relented, and the young couple married. Just as well, the minister's relative told me, or he wouldn't be around to tell the story!

There are so many fascinating stories connected to St Andrew's

Manly. Quite a few were told to me by Dr John Begg, the session clerk at St Andrew's during my time there.

Anyway, I am now back on track to tell you the ghost-cat story. I don't suppose there is a great deal to tell, but it concerns one of our children, who was in her twenties at the time.

She occupied a smaller room, as her bedroom which, we were told, had once been the maid's room, back in the days when just about every household had a maid or two. (I wonder if the maids had maids?)

One morning over breakfast our daughter said, 'I had the strangest experience last night! I felt a cat jump up on the bed and settle down near my feet. I could feel its weight. I was sure it wasn't Claude or Cynthia.' (Our cats. I was sure it wasn't one of them, because they had their own very comfortable quarters in the house at night, and I'd let them out earlier that morning).

'Anyway,' she said, 'just to be sure it wasn't either of those, I checked, and there was no cat in the room with me.'

The ghost cat often spent the night on Heather's bed and sometimes she said she could hear its purring. Heather loves cats, so ghost cat or live cat, Heather would be pleased to have it there.

Manly manse was not only a beautiful home; it was also beautiful in other ways. A cousin of mine from down Leeton way came to stay with us once and when she walked into the lounge room she stopped and said, 'What a beautiful feeling is in this room!'

Sometimes, when I was in the lounge room during an evening, sharing my beanbag with Claude, 'the wild bush cat' (as I called him, because I rescued him as a feral kitten from out of the bush in rural Queensland), I became aware that he was looking at something invisible to me. Anyone who loves and understands cats will know what I mean. He was suddenly alert, head forward, ears pricked forward a little the way they do when a cat is really interested in something. His head would move slightly in the direction of something he could see, but I couldn't. I used to watch, fascinated, wishing that I could see what he was staring at with such avid interest. (Don't tell me it could have been a flying insect or something. Claude would not give it a second glance). Maybe he could see the ghost cat. I hope so.

I've lost count of the people who, while in that lounge room, told me they saw a figure walk past one of the windows, but vanish before arriving at the next window, which is virtually beside it. I saw that odd phenomenon several times myself. The first time I expected the front doorbell to ring, and got up to greet whoever it was, for a path runs past the windows to the front door, but it never did ring and there never was anyone there.

A husband, a wife, a boy and a dog

Belinda told me the story of Bella, a much-loved family boxer who loved her, her husband and their young son Ben, devotedly and equally. She'd been with them for about nine years and they could not imagine life without her.

Unfortunately, the couple separated, but neither wanted to part with Bella. Eventually the matter was resolved. Bella spent the week with Belinda's ex-husband, while Belinda had her at the weekends. Flawed as the arrangement was, it worked reasonably well, although as Bella began to age, she seemed to be spending more time with Belinda's ex. The dog loved them all and seemed to be content to be with either family.

One night, Belinda told me, she woke, weeping bitterly for no apparent reason. She checked the time and discovered it was quite late at night - in fact very early in the morning, for it was about 3.00am. She was filled with a grief and melancholy she did not understand but finally, mystified, and still crying, she drifted back to sleep.

The morning brought the sad news. Her ex-husband rang to say that during the night, Bella had died. Although she'd been diagnosed with a heart murmur as a puppy, it had never been cause for alarm. In fact the vet had assured them that Bella was very fit for her age, so her death was almost totally unexpected. Belinda learned that Bella had died about the time she awoke, crying.

Belinda said that Bella was a very calm, gentle and intuitive dog. It was obvious, she said, that Bella fretted, wanting them all in the same place at the one time. Belinda suspects she also felt a lot of the heartache from the tears and pain of the marriage breakdown. 'She was the one who consoled us, her human family, through some very tough times,' she said.

There is a strange little addendum to the story. Belinda refrained from telling her son Ben the news of Bella's death until he got home from school. 'He heard me out, then said 'I know. Last night I dreamed Bella died.'

Belinda was astounded, but it was true. Since then I've had a chance to speak to Ben in person, and he confirmed what his mother said. 'It was so strange,' Ben told me, 'and so sad. That night, I dreamed that Bella and I were playing, just as we did of old, when we were both much younger, but she wasn't a young dog in my dream. She was the age she was the last time I saw her. All the same, it was marvellous! We played and chased and ran together, and both of us seemed so happy, so full of the joy of living, so happy to be in each other's company. Then I realised that underneath the outward joy was an elusive, underlying sadness, and in my heart I knew that Bella was dead. She'd come to me, to say goodbye.'

Belinda believes Ben's dream helped him to cope. 'He coped better than I did,' she said.

There is no rational explanation for such an amazing story, so full of pathos and mystery, except to conclude that spirit reached out to spirit - Bella's to Belinda's and to her son's. I felt deeply saddened as I listened to the story, and thought of sad earthly separations that don't involve death; when people we've loved have left to live somewhere else permanently, or we've left them. At the farewell party, there is jollity and laughter, but the underlying sadness that accompanies separations is just under the surface, just as it was in Ben's dream.

Sadly, Belinda's ex-husband, who had no warning or premonition of Bella's death, still grieves for her. He has never recovered from her death, and we can understand that, and feel for him in his grief.

There are countless stories of the spiritual connection between humans and animals. It seems to me that although Bella appeared to be happy enough, she fretted that the family members weren't together. It's sad to think that she had no way of conveying that information.

There are four words in the Greek language that are translated as 'love' but each refers to a different kind of love, such as filial (family) love, or erotic love, and so forth. The Greek word used throughout the New Testament for spiritual love is *agapé*, (pronounced agarpay). It's the love that breaks down all barriers - powerful enough to survive death. It's the love that never dies. There is no completely accurate translation into English, which uses the one word for 'love.' St Paul in his First Letter to the Corinthians, chapter 13, wrote that in time, everything will pass away, but faith, hope and love will remain. Of those great spiritual virtues, the greatest is love [*agapé*]. *Love never fails*, continued the Apostle. The story of Bella speaks of that sort of love, which is eternal. Who can possibly think that animals don't have a soul?

The man who delayed his own death

When I was in the Army and living in WA, there was a phone call from a lady who told me that her husband was dying. He'd been discharged from the Army on medical grounds, and they both wanted to see me.

When I went to their home, Angus was still well enough to tell me the horrible story. He was a Scot who'd decided some years before to migrate to Australia. He arrived as a young man and started to look for work. 'There's work for you up north of here,' he was told, 'called Wittenoom. They mine blue asbestos up there and they're looking for workers.'

Angus was 'footloose and fancy free' as the saying has it, so decided to give it a try.

At Wittenoom he discovered that his job was loading the blue asbestos into bags and shaking it down. Large quantities of asbestos dust billowed up in his face as he shook the bags.

Accepting the position at Wittenoom was accepting a death warrant.

These days everyone knows the horrible truth concerning asbestos and the tragic consequences of many of those who come into contact with it.

Angus was there only a few short weeks before deciding that it wasn't the life for him, so moved south and in time joined the Australian Army and was posted back to WA. He married Julie and had a lovely little family comprising his wife, a couple of children and a dear little dog that was very much a part of the family. 'Buttons' slept at the end of the couple's bed each night.

Angus became sick and the diagnosis was tragic: asbestosis, or technically, mesothelioma, the lung disease caused by minute particles of asbestos, for which there is no cure.

Angus realised he was dying and immediately filed a compensation claim so that his family would be cared for after his death. I don't know what went on regarding the claim but I do know that an enormous legal battle was fought at the time over Angus's claim and other claims associated with asbestosis. All the indications were that Angus would die before the matter was resolved and Julie feared that she and the children would be left to struggle on with no financial help.

I could do nothing on the legal side, which was in the hands of lawyers, but I spent a lot of time over many days, with Angus and the family as he grew weaker. When it was realised death was possibly no more than hours away, Angus was taken to hospital. Still he refused to die, despite all the confident medical predictions of 'an hour or so.'

The medical people were amazed at Angus's refusal to succumb.

Some time within that week, Julie had word: the courts had granted compensation of a very large sum of money to Angus.

Overjoyed, Julie rushed to the hospital and told him the good news.

He smiled, too weak to do anything else. Now, knowing his family was safe, he could let go. He died later that same day.

Despite its sadness, it's really a remarkable story of a man whose love for his wife and family was such that he refused to die until he was assured they would be cared for.

Now here is the odd part. The day after the funeral, Julie rang me: 'Lachlan – you must see this – come as soon as you can!'

I left almost at once. When I arrived, Julie told me the reason for the call: little Buttons, their dog who slept at the end of their bed every night, refused to enter the room. It wasn't a grieving thing. He stood at the door of the room, barking, staring at something she could not see, but he could.

Was Angus in there? I don't know, but it was very odd. One theory I've heard over the years is that our spirits do not immediately leave, or maybe some spirits or souls don't leave immediately. There's no point in asking me – I don't know. I'll just have to wait until it's my turn, and you your turn, to find out.

The following year, a new Commandant; a Brigadier in rank, was posted to 5MD (WA). He was a fine man, and his wife was very pleasant too. They were our neighbours in Fremantle. The Commandant's house was really lovely, surrounded by many trees and was known as 'Gun House.' Our house next door was known as 'Rifle Cottage' but it was certainly more than a cottage. It was large, and classified by the National Trust, but of course nowhere near the size and elegance of the Commandant's house, which was also classified. They had a dog, and our dog Bonnie, a border collie, somehow used to leap about five feet up the fence and hang over it, balancing there, so that she could bark at the Commandant's dog.

If you haven't gone to sleep by now, I just wanted to make the point that the commandant decided to visit the far-flung, northern outposts of 5MD, where there were numerous Army Reserve units. He decided to acquaint some of his senior officers with what lay up there, and as I was the senior chaplain 5MD he asked me to go too. The conversation went something like this: 'I'll be visiting some of the A-Res units north of here next week padre. You'll be going too. Pack your bags. We'll be away a few days. You'll get a signal with the joining instructions.' That is the usual way brigadiers 'ask' their staff to do things. That's just the way it is, and always has been, and I for one hope it stays that way.

We travelled by air, in a RAAF Caribou (pictured). The local Caribou squadron was known among the RAAF and other troops as 'Black Duck Airlines,' which was appropriate for WA. It was an interesting trip and we stayed overnight at various A-Res drill halls, sleeping on camp stretchers.

(Did I just hear you mumble 'Why are you telling me all this stuff?'). Well, I'm telling you 'all this stuff' as you so eloquently put it, because the Commandant decided he'd like to take a look at Wittenoom on the way back, so we landed there, on the old airstrip.

It's now a ghost town and when we landed and had a look about, a few of us shuddered. A dry wind blew among a desolation of abandoned buildings and ramshackle sheds. Open doors creaked and groaned and banged in the wind. An atmosphere of misery hung in the very air. I was glad when the brigadier decided he'd seen enough.

Since then I've heard that people, probably wanting to live in the abandoned houses, have moved back in. As far as I'm concerned, they're welcome to it.

Aliens, or What?

10

'Spaceships'

Watch out! Watch out!
There are spaceships about!
I saw one last night
In the pale moonlight
As it whizzed out of Mars
And zoomed past the stars,
Then came down to the ground
Without any sound
And a little fellow
(bright green and yellow)
Jumped out of that ship
With a hop and a skip
And asked me if I'd
Like to take a joy ride
In his stellar sledge
To the galaxy's edge
Where in a café
On the far Milky Way
He'd buy me a treat
Of space dishes to eat.
He jerked his green thumb
Which clearly meant 'come'
But I turned and I ran
From that strange little man
As fast as I could
Back home through the wood
Where I hid in my bed
Sheet over my head
And scared out of my wits
Chewed my blanket to bits!
Mum thinks I'm a scream
And says it's a dream,
But I know it's true
So I'm telling you:
Beware! Take care!!
There are spaceships out there!

Lachlan Ness

That's a little ditty that popped into my head when a couple of our children were little, so I worked on it, and when it was right, jotted it down for them. They still love it. I've often thought it would be a great children's book, if the right artist thought so too – couple of lines to a brightly coloured page, but so far nothing's happened

The 'Flying Saucers' of Woomera

I've never seen a UFO but I've heard some interesting stories from some very credible people. When I was in the Army and posted to a unit in Melbourne, the OC's secretary was a very pleasant lady whose husband had retired as an officer in the RAAF, so they'd moved around a lot too.

One of their postings was to Woomera, in South Australia. It was back in the 1950s, she said, during the time of the atomic experiments out there.

Her husband told her that during the atomic bomb experiments, he and others could see strange, saucer-shaped, stationary objects in the distance, very high in the sky. No one had any idea what they were. Many photographs were taken of them of course, but the strange thing is, when they were developed, there was nothing to be seen. They were invisible to cameras.

'How the moon gets back home'

Here is an amusing little extract from a letter I received from my brother Peter in Melbourne, who has an amazing memory. He told me that one evening he and I stood in a paddock on the old farm in Leeton, observing a strange, glowing object, passing across the sky from south to north. We were only little. The only way he knows the south-north direction is because he recalls its course over our house.

He remembers thinking to himself: 'Oh – so that's how the moon gets back home!'

Neither of us had seen anything like it before. Apparently I'd instructed him, after it was out of sight, never to mention it to anyone, ever – and he never did, until he revived that ancient memory. For the life of me, I can't imagine why I told him not to tell anyone. An even greater mystery is the fact that he took notice and never did tell anyone!

That Night in Mirrabooka

by VN and JW

Take a look at the following letter I received a few weeks ago from a friend of mine. I won't show you any letters unless I know the person in question. By the way, if you find the light in this room is a bit low to read by, just turn on that table lamp beside you... that's better...

'I almost dropped the frying pan, hot with lamb cutlets. I stood looking out the kitchen window, unable to believe my eyes. I called my partner and he looked too. We rushed outside. It was just on dark, about eight pm, on a clear night, and there above us was a flying saucer!

I know you'll think I'm a weirdo, a nut job, but I swear it's true. We lived in Mirrabooka, Lake Macquarie, NSW. It was about 1983. I'm saying that year because my daughter saw it too and she was about five years old. She remembers it, but thinks we lived in a different house. Don't discount her opinion however; she's a Taurus – well grounded, and an accountant, who sees things quite clearly. And she also saw our very own UFO.

It looked like your typical, everyday sort of UFO. A shiny, silvery disk with five circular bright lights underneath, and I mean searchlight bright. It stayed for a while, minutes anyway, and did what any self-respecting flying saucer would do. It hovered. Truly, in the ultimate definition of hover, the UFOs have it hands down. It took off straight up into the air and disappeared. We drew a picture straight away, and both agreed we saw the same thing. Just as we were calming down we heard the sound of screaming jets coming from the north. There were three fighter planes and they headed in the direction of the now vanished UFO. By this time, dinner was the last thing to worry about, so the burnt offering didn't bother our little family.

Next day was the test of my credibility. Should I tell others what we had seen, or not? I didn't get a chance to bring it up first, because when I went to work the first person I saw was a butcher. He was big, brawny and very matter of fact. On this day though, he was keen to lead the conversation about the UFO. He'd drawn it, yes, on a piece of butcher paper. IT WAS EXACTLY THE SAME AS MINE! Next person I met was a young man known for his colourful delusions about spacemen. And he had a drawing too. EXACTLY LIKE IT WAS - EXACTLY THE SAME AS MINE!

He gave the same story and of course with his history of invention most laughed at him and his fanciful tale, until I produced my own pen and ink proof. Now I was put into the Looney category too, but I knew what I'd seen was real. The story went nowhere for several months until the day I was invited to join a group visit to Williamtown RAAF base. We were privileged to look at the amazing radar room and speak to some technicians. I told one chap my story and he laughed. I asked could he look up the date (it was still fresh in my mind then). He did and shut it down so fast I knew something had happened. I saw the words 'Authorised Personnel Only' on the screen. He looked very smart in his uniform, but could I trust him? Nope. I pressured him a little, I mean here I was having a chance in a million to check for proof of the thing, shiny and light bright, that we'd seen zap past us into the night sky. The technician acknowledged there'd been some jets on a training mission that day. Then he said the radar units sometimes have glitches, and the jets went out anyway for training practice. On the night I saw the flying foreigner, the computer was noted to have shown an insect across the inside of the screen. What! Is that even possible? I think he said the first thing he thought of, and the grin he gave me proved it. So to this day my daughter and I maintain the Mirrabooka sky was alive with aliens and RAAF heroes, playing chasies with one another across our peaceful Lake Macquarie skies.'

UFOs over Gloucester

When John Easton, his cousin Ian and their friend Noel Herbert left to spend a weekend camping up in the hills around Gloucester, NSW, they had no idea what awaited them – in more ways than one. The three are great friends, and John attends the same church that Janet and I do, and it was while having morning tea after the service one Sunday that John told me this very unusual story.

He said that he and the others had decided to spend the weekend on a camping trip, which they liked to do from time to time. He had returned from a business meeting in Sydney before heading up with the others into the hill country of Gloucester. John loves that country, for he grew up on a 640 acre dairy farm up that way, at Belbora, near Krambach.

Before they left, he looked at the sky and debated whether or not they should go, for the sky was heavily clouded and jet-black. The threat of a big storm hung in the still warm air.

Finally, they decided to take the risk, and headed off, and in time arrived at their camping spot, down Belbora Creek Road, about three kilometres from the main road. It was a significant spot for John, for it was the place where the old family homestead once stood.

They had barely enough time to erect the tents before the storm crashed in on them, driven by a wild gale, accompanied by thunder, lightning and massive hail stones.

Finally, the storm moved on, and as so often happens after a great storm like that, it left behind a beautifully clear, still, starry night. Half a kilometre away was a hill, freshly washed by the storm, silhouetted against the night sky.

The friends lit the campfire and sat around it, yarning and enjoying their billy tea and coffee. John pulled out his mouth organ and gave them a tune or two.

Suddenly Noel called out, 'Look – what's that?' They looked.

Between them and the hill the astonished men saw two objects, travelling in tandem at great speed, parallel to the ground, at an altitude of approximately three hundred metres or a bit more.

'It was amazing,' John told me. 'They looked like rifle bullets, (but much bigger of course), and each appeared to have something like an after-burner, with plumes of flame blazing behind. What really amazed us however was the silence. These things, whatever they were, flew in complete silence – there wasn't the slightest sound to indicate their presence – it was just by chance that Noel looked up and saw them and called out to us. Next thing, they had disappeared behind the hill. About twenty minutes later, a couple of jet fighters, probably from Williamtown RAAF Base, screamed overhead. We supposed they had been scrambled. Later, however, when I rang the RAAF Base to report what we'd seen, they denied that there had been any RAAF activity up there during the evening.'

'It's an amazing story, John. Was that the end of it?'

'No – but first, do you mind if I add a touch of Steven Spielberg?' John asked with a grin.

Of course I was all ears. 'Please – carry on!'

'Well,' he said, 'next morning we went off to do a bit of hiking among the hills, where we saw something I'd never seen before; nor had the others – and I grew up on a dairy farm. It was a dead cow in a creek – but the odd thing is, the cow was standing upright, dead! Of course, after the previous night's experience it was only natural for us to make up all sorts of stories as to how the cow had died and yet somehow remained standing.'

'And so you never heard any more concerning those UFOs?'

'Funny you should ask!' said John. 'Noel knew someone who was in the control room that night at Williamtown RAAF Base. About a year later, when Noel mentioned the incident, his friend told him that jet fighters were indeed scrambled that night. By the way, there's one more thing: the three of us decided to draw what we saw, and then compare the drawings. When we did so, we discovered that they were virtually identical. I'll see if I can find mine – I'm sure I have it somewhere. Would you like to see it?. Would I ever! 'Please!'

As it turned out, John was happy to photocopy his original drawing for me, as well as another, that one of the others had drawn, and he is also prepared to let me show them to you. It's here somewhere – wait a minute... (Scrabble-scrabble, complete with various mutterings). It's here, somewhere... (vaguely, accompanied by head-scratching). We'll look for it later. (You'll find all the photos and things in a pile over there, in that folder).

The strange case of the Nullarbor lights

Here's an interesting letter from our friend Wendy...

'Tom and I have a niece whose name is Claire. She is married to David, who at that time was in the Australian Army and based in Townsville, Queensland.

They had driven over to Perth with their large Italian mountain dog for a family gathering and were on their way back to Queensland, travelling across the Nullarbor. They had to stop for the night and were equipped with a tent and some camping gear. David was busy putting up the tent when he noticed that the dog was becoming very agitated. That was most unusual, for the dog was very intelligent and well-disciplined. The dog continued to whine, so David looked out from the tent into the darkness and saw an amazing sight: there were dozens of lights in amongst the trees outside their tent. By this time the dog was very distressed. David, alarmed at the dog's behaviour, called out to Claire to pack up everything, because they were moving at once. She had no idea what the problem was, but David in his wisdom took some photos of the lights. They packed up and moved a few kilometres down the road and set up for the night. The dog was completely docile and there was no reaction at all.

Wendy's story continues:

'In 2010 Tom and I travelled across the Nullarbor and stopped at a truckies' stop for the night. We went to the little bar to have a drink before dinner and began chatting to the other people sitting there. In the course of the conversation, I told the story of the lights in the trees and one of the men said 'take a look at the wall behind you.' When I looked, I was amazed to see newspaper cuttings of identical and other sightings on the Nullarbor at various times over a period of years. It seems Claire, David and their dog were not alone in seeing the mysterious lights, and the dog's reaction seemed to indicate a sinister presence. Even reading of the reports on the wall gave me a very strange and eerie feeling.'

Something to think about...

If you ask me if I believe in UFOs and so on, I can tell you that I do, based on the evidence of what is not said, as much as what is said. I mean, if there's no truth in some of those stories, one would have to ask why governments and their departments keep hiding information?

Admittedly, files have been made available, but many with large sections blacked out 'for security reasons.' I don't know about you, but when a government, or anybody for that matter, says it is hiding nothing while keeping its hand figuratively behind its back, I am a bit suspicious.

A classic case in recent years were the mysterious lights in the skies above NZ. The Australian TV journalist, Quentin Fogarty had been sent to NZ to check out the story. His team hired an aircraft, piloted by a Captain Startup. While the aircraft was airborne, the lights began circling all around the aircraft. It was at night, so little could be seen, although the team on board were photographing them. Meanwhile on the ground the UFO lights were plainly visible on NZ radar. It was quite an amazing spectacle.

From what I recall, the film was sent to the UK (or somewhere) to be analysed. I remember reading in the newspapers later that according to some expert, the lights were no more than lights being reflected off clouds from fishing boats offshore! I can't say I believed that one.

There are literally thousands, of sightings each year for which there is no plausible explanation, and from what I understand, the number of sightings is increasing; especially in the light of more modern photographic equipment. It seems to me that governments are hooked on hiding the truth from us – 'to avoid world-wide panic,' I believe is the story. Of course, there are alarmists among us, as well as conspiracy theorists everywhere, and here's a story I can pass on.

When we lived in Oakey Qld, on the base at the Army Aviation Centre, a lady in Oakey's main street, noting I was in military uniform, asked me about the big hangar at the workshops battalion where the Aviation Corps aircraft were maintained, repaired and so on. 'Would you be able to tell me about the crashed UFO in that hangar?' she asked.

I was completely taken aback. I'd not heard of that rumour. 'I'm in that hangar several times a week. I can assure you there is no crashed UFO, and no little alien corpses, green, grey or otherwise,' I told her. She passed me a look. 'Of course. You'd have to say that, wouldn't you?' (Nudge-nudge-wink-wink). Why we have to have an Australian Roswell and 'Hangar 18' equivalent is beyond me.

The Oakey UFO

There is however, a strange little personal story associated with Oakey, and UFOs. One of our sons, (a teenager at the time) used to enjoy a stroll on a hot evening, from our married quarter on the base out along a quiet country road for a mile or two, to the civilian airstrip, which is not far from the military airstrip. He came back one evening with a mystifying story. He said on the way home he saw what appeared to be a 'ball of light' in the sky, completely silent, approaching the civilian airstrip. Whatever it was, it wasn't expected, because the landing strip lights weren't on. It appeared to be preparing to land. He estimated it to be not far above treetop level at the time. Suddenly it changed direction, climbed and disappeared at very high speed – soundlessly. Oakey civilian airstrip is very small and is not lit up at night unless an aircraft is due to land, which isn't often, so he wasn't confusing it with some aircraft light or associated light. In fact neither airstrip had its lights on for a night-time landing. If he were given to daydreams of that nature, the story would not be told. He happens to be of a serious disposition and apart from his family, I don't think he told anyone else. The Oakey civilian strip wasn't used very often during our time there. Sometimes it was used when the commercial airport at Toowoomba was fogged in – not uncommon in winter. In fact it so happened that one morning word came to the Base that Mr Joh Bjelke Peterson, the Premier of Queensland had arrived, expecting to land his aircraft at Toowoomba, but it was closed because of fog and he was diverted to Oakey. Some of the Aviation Corps officers met the premier when he landed and took him off to the officers' mess for a cuppa and toast until the fog lifted. They enjoyed chatting to Joh, but finally word came that the fog had lifted and Joh (who flew himself about) would be able to land at Toowoomba. The officers escorted him back to the airstrip. As Joh was walking over to his aircraft he turned and addressed his hosts: 'You've all done very well!' Joh, it seems, had a humorous streak and also liked to watch the British TV comedy, 'Are you being served?'

Yes, I know that story has nothing to do with ghosts and bump in the night things, but a bit of levity here and there won't hurt, and after all, this is a fireside chat that includes other true stories, and that's when all sorts of conversational things are permitted to pop up!

Now, where was I...? Oh yes... UFOs. The world's history, back to its earliest days contains all sorts of stories associated with mysterious flying craft. If you find it hard to believe, Google the strange 'foo fighters' of World War Two that used to fly alongside allied aircraft.

Even some of the astronauts claim to have seen 'bogies' (UFO's) or believe in their existence. I think they called them 'bogies.' The highly decorated US Navy captain and astronaut Edgar Mitchell comes to mind. He was the sixth astronaut to land on the moon and says openly that he is '90 percent sure' that many of the thousands of UFOs, recorded since the 1940s, belong to visitors from other planets. That is an amazing claim from a man with such a high public profile.

Rick, a friend of mine for many years and an elder in his Church, spent his career in the RAAF and retired as a squadron leader. When Rick was young airman back about 1970, he worked in Air Defence control. Years ago, I recall he told me that somewhere around that time, when based in Darwin, he saw something very interesting on his radar screen. It was an object travelling from north-west to south-east 'in excess of 5,000 miles an hour (8,000kph) and in excess of 50,000 feet.'

'Could it have been any natural thing?' I asked.

'Such as?'

'A satellite?'

He shook his head. 'Wrong direction for a satellite,' he said, 'and it was certainly not a flock of birds! It went from one side of the radar screen to the other and disappeared. Anyway, I reported it to the supervisor, who told me to forget it. There's no way anyone could possibly discover what it was, so I did what he told me to do – I forgot about it.'

Angels or Aliens?

'The day was hot and pregnant with the threat of a storm; the year, somewhere in the early nineteen seventies; the place, the road beside the Hawkesbury River just to the east of the hamlet of Spencer; The car an Austin Kimberley; the occupants, a youngish married couple...'

That's the opening sentence of a rather intriguing story told to me by a friend of mine, whom I shall call Mac. (I have several friends called Mac).

He and his wife were travelling on that section of the road when, as they rounded a bend they came across a couple, roughly their age, who appeared to be in need of help. Mac obligingly pulled up to see if he could be of assistance, but all they wanted was a lift to Peats

Ridge. Mac was only too willing to oblige, for it was on their way.

On arrival, the young couple thanked Mac and his wife profusely, and left. As they walked away Mac checked the rear seat of the car in case anything had been left behind. Nothing had, but he noticed something immediately that astounded him, and, he confessed to me, filled him with a degree of unease.

The Austin's seats were made of open foam, he told me, and whenever anyone sat in the rear bench seat, it was impossible not to leave an indent where one's rump had been. The depressions remained for approximately fifteen minutes after someone had exited the car, before air slowly expanded them again to their normal shape.

Now, half a minute after his rear seat passengers had departed, Mac looked at the spot where there should have been two deep and distinct depressions, and saw none – but the couple had been sitting there for about an hour. Mac assured me such a thing had never happened before, and it never happened again.

Mac is an engineer by profession, and knew his car. The lack of depressions in the seat has him stymied; especially in view of the fact that he saw the couple in his rear vision mirror, sitting comfortably... 'I wonder,' he mused when we discussed it, 'if perhaps my wife and I entertained angels unawares?'

He was quoting the Letter to the Hebrews 13:2. They may well have been. I feel puzzled by this story, which at first may seem a little mundane, but the more one dwells on it, the odder it becomes. I have great faith in Mac's judgement regarding anything of a practical nature. If he said the seat would not return to its normal shape for about fifteen minutes, you can be assured that it was so. It may not have been the same on all Austin Kimberleys, but it was on his. At first I debated using this story, but upon reflection I remembered a chair we had in my parents' house. It was an old leather chair and when one exited it, invariably an indentation was left. It took some time before the squeezed-out air returned with an audible sigh – which I always thought of as an expression of relief. It was impossible not to leave an indentation. Occasionally, one reads of people who claim that there are 'visitors' in our midst, who walk around as we do and give every appearance of being human, but are not. They are aliens, is the claim. Perhaps Mac and his wife were entertaining angels – but who knows?

The lights of Dunedoo

An article in the *Sun-Herald* dated 27 January 2013 caught my eye.

The article, headed 'More than a Starry, Starry Night' included the picture of a young man looking into the heavens at mysterious-looking objects. It was quite eye-catching. It was the name 'Dunedoo' however that really made me take another look, for the parish of Coolah-Dunedoo, NSW, was where I spent about three months some time previously, working as a locum minister for the Presbyterian Church.

When I finished reading the article I was quite intrigued, for the young man (Damien Nott) who was interviewed by a 'Sun-Herald' journalist told of strange lights that he was filming over his farm just about every night of the week. The journalist wrote that his crew had filmed two lights moving in tandem across the sky at high altitude. In the article he wrote that Airservices Australia and Sydney Observatory said 'it was likely they were satellites.'

I don't know about anyone else, but I find it rather offensive when various people or bodies, official or otherwise, make pronouncements based on statements made second, third or even more-hand.

Damien Nott responded by saying that he knew what satellites were. As he and the journalist watched, the objects changed speed and direction and also changed colour. 'That's not the behaviour of a satellite,' said Damien.

I think I make reference somewhere else to an official pronouncement made by someone without seeing a thing, or even seeming to understand that in the case in question, the objects were being tracked on radar. UFO debunkers are among the worst offenders here I think.

The article in the 'Sun-Herald' reported that Mariana Flynn, the president of UFO Research NSW had also gone to Dunedoo to check out Mr Nott's story and told the journalist she believes that Damien is quite genuine. I know that UFO research people are careful, for their cause is not helped at all by hoaxers, people who make natural errors, or crackpots. In Scotland I once photographed the ruins of an ancient castle, while behind it thirteen miles out to sea were two oil rigs. I used a telephoto lens. It was the contrast I wanted to capture: the ruins of a 14th century castle and in the same frame, modern oil rigs. When I looked at the scene on the computer, I was intrigued to see what looked like a UFO that I hadn't been able to observe with the naked eye. Intrigued, I emailed the photo off to a UK UFO research body, just to be sure. The reply came back: It's a bird. The distance had corrupted the image, making it look like a possible UFO. It's easy to make mistakes, which is why UFO research bodies such as UFO Research NSW play an important role in identifying true from false.

I made a point of contacting both Ms Flynn and Damien by phone and email.

When she was at Dunedoo, Ms Flynn said, they saw up to nine objects in the night sky, and while some could be discounted as satellites, others certainly could not. Objects that change shape and colour, that change course, speed up and slow down, can hover and then accelerate from stationary to enormous speed, are not satellites; nor are they conventional aircraft.

I made a point of looking at some of the YouTube material that Damien has, and it looks very real to me. If anyone can prove otherwise, I'd be very surprised to learn it. He has no reason to lie. I had (and have) the impression that he is a very honest, down-to-earth person who is looking for answers, and getting nowhere. While some may regard him as a crackpot, others are taking him more seriously, including, I believe, some people possibly aligned to security services - but that's unofficial. Forget I said that. It's lucky we're in the room alone... apart from Tonkie and Jock, our cat and dog, who, won't say anything. They're both asleep anyway.

A growing number of people in Dunedoo and elsewhere are paying more attention these days to what may be hovering overhead. It's intriguing. Why is there apparent official secrecy in some countries? I remember Mr Obama declaring that if he was elected president (the first time) he'd open the UFO files to the public. We're still waiting Mr Obama, even Down Under. (I promise not to get hysterical if I learn something unusual).

I have been in contact with Damien on several occasions. He told me that four police officers around the Dubbo and Orange areas, and one in Sydney, have been in contact with him and have stated that they have seen UFOs but are not willing to face ridicule, so are keeping silent.

Damien has sent me some amazing material. One is of two mysterious objects seen near a commercial aircraft vapour trail. You can now see that one on YouTube. It seems that reports of UFO activity have been increasing rapidly around the world, many from reliable sources. What is happening?

I know that Damien has the support of several UFO organizations in Australia and abroad. Others around the world have examined his footage and declared it genuine. If I thought he was a hoaxer, he would not be getting coverage here. To make up your own mind, go to Damien's YouTube video. He is more than happy for you to do so. Type in knightoftruth79.

You may well discover some interesting information that will give you something to think about.

... and other true stories

UFO Activity over Nowra

One evening in 1954, a Navy pilot, returning to the Naval Base at Nowra NSW, radioed that his Sea Fury aircraft had two unidentified objects keeping pace with him; one each side of his plane. The Base's radar technicians observed the objects on their screens. The UFOs finally departed at high speed, but it left the pilot shaken. Lots of questions were asked over the next few weeks, but no answers could be provided. The incident had wide media coverage. As usual, when the UFO questions are put to our masters in Canberra or wherever, despite all the evidence of reliable witnesses, such as pilots and other responsible citizens, invariably they look blank and reply 'UFO? What UFO?'

We wind the clock on, to 1973. About 2.30am one January morning of that year, a lady whom I'll call Elizabeth was driving her car northwards, from Durras South on the South Coast of NSW to the family campsite at Shoalhaven Heads, NSW. With her were her husband, their two teenage daughters Jenny and Robyn, and a family friend Trevor, who was a corporal in the Army, all of whom (apart from the driver of course) were dozing. She knew that somewhere among that pile of people was the family dog, Scampy, who doubtless was also sleeping.

Somewhere near the Sussex Inlet turn-off, Elizabeth saw a very bright light ahead. It appeared to be very high, and she assumed it was something like a truck or semi-trailer coming down a high hill towards them.

Astonishment gripped her when suddenly the object appeared to be very close. For a brief moment she thought it was a plane crashing, but it was very much under control as a huge craft took up a position somewhere out to the left of the car, keeping pace with it. Alarmed, Elizabeth called out to the others: 'Look at that! What do you think it is?' At once they were all wide awake, staring at the object.

The soldier, Trevor, who was seated on the left in the back seat, stared at it intently.

'That's no ordinary aircraft,' he exclaimed; 'It's a UFO!'

Elizabeth said that the UFO's appearance was as many are described. It was circular, with a dome on top. The bright light she'd seen earlier was on the bottom of the craft, still emitting a powerful white light. She could see a row of portholes along the side, and Trevor called out that he could see figures looking out at them. Under the portholes was a row of red lights, and as the occupants of the car looked, they began to blur, to form what appeared to be a ribbon of red, as if the part below the portholes was starting to rotate very quickly.

The UFO kept pace with the car for about twenty kilometres past the Sussex Inlet turn-off. Suddenly, in a heartbeat of time, it shot upwards. Elizabeth stopped the car, so Trevor jumped out to get a better look. 'I can just see it!' he told them. 'It's now very high, over the water.' Then it was gone.

One important fact they noted as they discussed the incident later was the UFO's silence – so silent that it didn't even wake Scampy the dog. None in the car heard any sound coming from the UFO.

The following day, Trevor wrote a full report of the incident. He, Elizabeth and the others took it to the Base and were escorted to the Base Commander's office.

They expected to see only the Commander, but several senior Naval officers were with him. Elizabeth and the others were questioned closely and at length, and it was obvious that their story was treated very seriously. They learned that many others had contacted the Naval Base about the UFO.

Trevor's report was filed and he was told that he was not to speak of the incident publicly while he remained in the Army.

When Elizabeth returned to work some time later, she mentioned the story to one of her colleagues who was English, and had served in the Royal Navy years before. He heard her out, then told her of an incident that had happened when he was serving aboard one of the Royal Navy's Polaris submarines.

'We were on exercise,' he said, 'and our submarine was on the surface when the sonar pinged something on the sea bottom that should not have been there, so we challenged it. Of course we assumed that it was probably a Russian submarine, for those were the Cold War years. Before our astonished eyes however, a UFO shot out of the sea in front of us and disappeared into the clouds.'

Elizabeth's story is amazing, and equally so is the story of her colleague. I have not the slightest doubt that both stories are true. I wish I could capture something of the graphic way Elizabeth told the story to Janet and me (and to Jock, but he didn't appear very interested) one day recently over tea and cake in her sunny kitchen

'The great pity,' Elizabeth continued, 'is that few believe me, and I don't lie about anything, let alone stories like that. Even my own church friends refuse to believe me. They don't want to hear about it and laughingly ask me what I've been drinking. They probably don't realise it, but not only are they calling me a liar; they're calling my family, who also saw the UFO, liars too. Our daughters are still a little traumatised about that UFO incident, all these years later'

If you want to read confirmation of this story, and have access to the Internet, Google Nowra UFO and you'll find it. We're just fortunate enough to know Elizabeth.

It's really funny (as in odd, rather than amusing), how so many people refuse to believe what others say, when it falls outside their own life experience, and here's a good example: I recall reading somewhere that during the American Civil War, the Union Army was supplied with new rifles that had a far longer range than the old rifles they'd been using.

A Confederate Army General stood up in a trench to see what was happening, and one of his troops told him to get his head down, warning him of the long range accuracy of the Union rifles.

'Don't be silly!' the General is reported to have replied, 'They could never fire a round this fa-'

... and other true stories

Mistaken Identities and some more head scratchers

11

Be sure of your facts

The following is part of a letter I received from a lady whose name is Joan.

She and her husband are good friends of ours and live in country NSW. In her letter, Joan recalls an experience that occurred when she was a young girl. The earlier part of the letter refers to a time she spent in NZ with some other members of her family. I found her letter to be most interesting indeed:

'...After returning to Australia, I stayed again with my aunt on her sheep property for a little while. The family who were managing the property for my aunt gave me a beautiful little puppy, a border collie, which I took home to our property, 'Eden.' I named the puppy Whisky. Dad and I trained him to become a working sheep dog.

One day Dad and Whisky went out to muster a mob of sheep into the yards. I was doing some work in the house at the time, but Dad asked me if I would help when he and Whisky got the sheep up to the yards. I knew he'd need someone there to open and close gates, as well as be prepared for anything else that may happen.

Some time later I heard unmistakable sounds of a mob of sheep approaching. I could hear sheep baahing, Whisky barking, Dad whistling and calling to Whisky: 'Go way back!'

When I looked outside, I was astonished to find nothing in sight! Not a sheep, no Whisky, no Dad, no dust.

I could hardly believe my eyes. How was it possible to hear all that, and yet see nothing? I went back inside, greatly puzzled and not long after, heard the same sound of approaching sheep and men and dogs and went out to help, but found nothing in sight...'

I'm going to leave the story there briefly and take you forward to another time and another place; this time in WA, about the year 1988...

I was a chaplain in the Army in those years. One day when I walked into an orderly room at Campbell Barracks, Swanbourne, WA,. a warrant officer called me over. 'I've a story you'll enjoy padre. Grab a cup of coffee, sit down and listen to this.' I did so. I knew the warrant officer quite well and knew the story would be a good 'un. I was not mistaken.

'I'm just back from leave, padre – rode my motor bike across the Nullarbor plains to visit some of the family interstate. The bike I have now is big, motor-wise, and in fact it's the most powerful motorbike available in Australia at present. There's no better place than the Nullarbor to try it out, so on the way back I opened her up, and besides, I was keen to get home. I'd been sitting on something over 200kph for about an hour, not thinking of much. I had the radio on, listening to some music through the headphones, when suddenly, a voice spoke to me, as clear as I'm talking to you. It came in through the headphones and over the music, and it said quite urgently, 'Slow down, you fool – slow down... Slow down you fool – slow down!' I looked ahead along the road. It was empty. I looked behind. Nothing... an empty road and a voice in my ears, warning me, possibly to save my life. Only God, or one of His angels, could do that. I slowed down and looked up to thank Him...'

Now I'm going to finish off the first story, then the one I just told you, and then I am going to tell you what it's all about. Here we go back to that quiet sheep property in western NSW. I'll let Joan finish her story:

That particular day, when Dad went to muster the sheep, and I went out to help but found no Dad, no Whisky and no sheep, I could still hear the barking and baahing, the whistling and commands going on close by. It was amazing, and even a little scary.

I looked up into a tree in the garden, and – there was the source of all the ruckus! There were two magpies up there, imitating perfectly the baahing, barking, the whistling and Dad's voice, as if they were right next to me! It was astounding. At the time, we had those two magpies living near the house. Each year they would hatch two or three young ones and we fed them little pieces of cut up meat, which they took from our hands. They lived there for many, many years. I'd forgotten what amazing mimics magpies are.'

It's true. Many varieties of birds in the parrot family are known as extraordinary mimics, but magpies too possess the same remarkable ability. Australian magpies are wild native birds and it is illegal to keep them without official permission – which was not the case here, of course. Like so many wild birds and animals, they don't object to the handout, and at present I am organised each morning by four topknot pigeons that descend from nowhere as soon as I walk out of the back door. I keep some wild birdseed as a handout for them. They are so trusting, and run about my feet, busily gathering breakfast.

Now let's return to our warrant officer, hurtling across the Nullarbor at over 200kph on his motorbike with a mysterious voice overriding his earphones and the music he's listening to. 'Slow down, you fool!' He hears the voice coming through loud and clear, with not another vehicle in sight. Believing it's a divine message, the soldier slows down and raises his eyes to heaven to thank God.

What he sees in not empty sky, but a police highway patrol aircraft, with a police officer using a powerful megaphone!

'I gave them a wave and slowed down. For some reason they didn't book me,' the warrant officer concluded.

Why am I telling you these two stories? I can see puzzlement 'writ large' all over your countenance.

Well, the truth is, many of us are inclined to fall into the trap of believing there is a supernatural or paranormal reason behind everything we don't understand. If Joan had not looked into the tree and seen the magpies, she may well have been convinced it was a supernatural experience. The same applies to the warrant officer, who also looked up and saw the police aerial patrol, who thought at first it was a message from God.

In that vein, I must pass on an amusing little story I was told one afternoon recently while chatting to a funeral director. He was still chortling over an incident that had occurred earlier that day at a crematorium. 'A friend of mine is a maintenance man at the local crematorium,' he told me. 'One of his duties is to clean out the furnaces and do any repair work required inside. They're big enough for him to climb into. He was inside one of the furnaces this morning, doing some maintenance work. As he climbed out, all covered in grey dust from head to foot, a woman visitor being shown through the crematorium, saw what she presumed to be a ghost. She took one look at the grey apparition emerging from the furnace, uttered a piercing shriek and fainted on the spot!' It's best to look for a natural cause first, when something strange and/or apparently inexplicable happens to us. That way, if ever the supernatural or paranormal enters our lives, we'll be able to recognise it for what it is.

The strange story of a car that didn't break down

Years ago, the road between Araluen and Moruya in southern NSW was dirt, and the following incident occurred in the 1980s.

A friend of mine and his teenage son were driving along the section of road that runs beside the river, quite close to the bottom of the road down the mountain from Majors Creek.

It had been a pleasant and easy drive – until suddenly from somewhere under the car their ears were assailed by very expensive, mechanical sounds.

He and his son pulled in off the road and jumped out of the car to ascertain the damage. They were puzzled to find nothing apparently wrong. They were still scratching their heads when short minutes later, a school bus, coming from the other direction, hurtled around the corner at high speed, showering them with dust and rocks as it powered up the road.

With nothing apparently wrong with the car, they set off again, the car sounding its usual well-mannered, Holden self.

A short distance along, the road suddenly narrowed, with sharp bends, a cliff on one side and a drop to the river on the other.

As they recalled the speed of the bus as it hurtled recklessly past, they realized that, had that mysterious mechanical noise not interrupted their journey, they would have met the bus on that section of the road – no room to pass, little chance of stopping in time.

They shuddered as they realized how close they, and the occupants of the bus, had come to catastrophe.

My friend has often pondered the strange incident, when a car that wasn't broken down, broke down, but shortly after, miraculously wasn't broken down... an incident that probably saved his and his son's lives as well as other innocent lives, although they didn't know how many were on the bus. Maybe it was only the driver.

All we can really say is that God alone knows what He is doing.

In the Old Testament you can read the story of Ruth, a non-Jewish woman – a Moabitess who won the heart of the wealthy Boaz and became his wife. It's a story that had a future, hundreds of years ahead. People at the time may well have asked why Ruth was chosen, and not some good Jewish lass? If you are wondering, read the long genealogy in Matthew's Gospel chapter one, and you will read that it is down that long line that Jesus traces His ancestry.

God knows the end from the beginning. For all we know, there may have been someone who was prevented from death because God had plans, somewhere in the future, of which we know nothing – but even that is foolish conjecture. There is no answer available to us, unless we are prepared to put all these things down to mindless chance.

I don't believe in mindless chance; nor does my friend. I'm quite happy to leave all those things in the hands of Him to Whom a thousand years are like a day that is past, or a watch in the night. (Psalm 90:4).

A story of betrayal, followed by a message

This story is so sad as we contemplate the emotions of one who has found the meaning of the word 'Betrayal.' It's also a story of divine comfort. The following words are his:

'The occasion, a Sunday School picnic in the early nineteen nineties, the place a rocky sandstone hilltop on 'Highlands,' a property right on the Great Divide in the central tablelands of NSW.

Our man had just discovered that his wife of some twenty years had, several days before, 'been caught in the act,' as it were, by their sixteen year-old daughter. The miscreant was none other than the careers advisor and school counsellor for his daughter's high school. Our man was, to say the very least, most distraught, and had gone to the picnic, both to take his three children, and to have some time to try to come to grips with the torment and upheaval, not only in his life and family, but also within the local congregation of whom our (betrayed) man was the principal lay preacher, elder and clerk of the local Presbytery. This man, shattered by the events of the past week, sat on a rock some distance from the children, assorted parents and grandparents half-heartedly listening to the Sunday School Superintendent telling the assembly a Bible-based story. Gradually he became aware of a figure, translucent, and slightly luminescent between himself and the surrounding trees which could be seen behind the figure. Our man sat for some time, transfixed by what he was seeing, when finally a feeling of great peace came over him.

Suddenly he heard the figure speak to him: 'Be still, and know that I am God.' (*Be still, and know that I am God: I will be exalted among the heathen, I will be exalted in the earth. The LORD of hosts is with us; the God of Jacob is our refuge.* (Psalm 46:10,11)) It is of significance that no one else at the picnic made any comment about seeing or hearing anything out of the ordinary.

I believe that God reveals what He wants people to see, hear, experience. Two or more people may be present, but only one may hear, see, experience. A good example can be found in the Book of Acts chapter 9:1-9ff: Saul's conversion. It seems that those travelling with Saul heard sound, but did not see the light that flashed around Saul or hear what was said to him. Our man in this story is not saying that the figure he saw was God; rather the figure conveyed a message, in the text of the Psalm. Perhaps the mysterious figure was an angel. 'Angelos' in the Greek can mean 'angel' or 'messenger. Whoever was the bringer, the message brought peace and eventual healing.

'Through each perplexing path of life...'

Those words are from a hymn, *O God of Bethel*, one of the Scottish paraphrases, which can also be found in many hymn books. The words are attributed to Philip Doddridge and Michael Bruce, who both lived in the 18th century and sadly, died young. I think Michael Bruce was only in his twenties when he died, but Doddridge lived long enough to become rather famous in his day. Anyway, the lovely words are paraphrases of just three verses from Genesis 28:20-22, when Jacob makes a covenant with God, after he poured oil on the stone that had been his pillow. He called the place 'Bethel' which means in the Hebrew, 'House of God' (verse 18). In my opinion, the hymn-tune, 'Salzburg' written by the great 18th century German classical composer, Michael Haydn, suits the words best. The Haydn boys, Joe and Mick, who were brothers, are two of my favourite composers. In fact Mick was a good friend of 'Volfy' (Wolfgang) Mozart, whose music (like the music of so many of the great composers) is beautiful beyond words.

Yes – I can see that raised eyebrow and the quizzical expression! They're saying to me, 'Why are you telling me all this? You keep doing that all the time.'

It was that lengthy silence a few minutes ago... I think you had drifted off, and I would have too, if that sudden hiss and crackling in the burning log hadn't startled me. For some reason, I was thinking of the way that God sometimes intrudes into our lives, and we don't even realise it at the time. For instance, Jake (Jacob) was certainly dodgy, and he'd legged it from home because he'd stolen his brother Esau's blessing and birthright. Esau was a huntin' shootin' and fishin' type, handy with a bow and arrow; who probably read the ancient version of *Sporting Shooter* magazine. He was mad enough to take out his young brother, because of what he'd done, so young Jake prudently hit the track until his big brother had cooled off.

The amazing thing about that story is the way God had chosen Jacob all along, and it was the dream, and Jacob's promise in the covenant, that changed him – just as God intended.

Remember the story of the Emmaus Road in Luke's Gospel? There are the two disciples on the afternoon of the resurrection, on their way to Emmaus, unaware of the astonishing events that had taken place that morning in Jerusalem. They become aware of a stranger who has appeared beside them, but they don't recognise the risen Lord, until later. It's in Luke 28, from verse 13.

I was thinking just then, that one can see that story as an analogy of life itself. Behind the scenes, as we walk the dusty road of life, there is Someone beside us, directing our way.

The other day I was chatting to Robian. Remember her?– I mentioned her and her husband earlier. Anyway, she told me a lovely little story. It's not dramatic, but as I listened I thought of the way the events of our life are marked out for us, the way Jacob's was, but we don't always see it – may never do so.

Robian told me that when she sat her final school exams many years ago, in a country town, she was delighted to discover, when the results came out, that she'd done very well; enough to earn a scholarship to Teachers' College. Shortly afterwards, the family moved to another country town. Robian and her family waited for further word concerning her scholarship, but none was forthcoming. Finally, it transpired that when the family had moved, the Department of Education had not been notified, so had no idea how to contact her.

Robian's father packed her and her mother off to Sydney to get it sorted, and they stayed with a relative, Auntie Rae.

In Sydney they discovered they were only just in time, for it was the last day for enrolments, and there were only three positions left.

Robian and her mother then discovered something else very exciting: they learned that Robian had also won a Commonwealth scholarship to go to University! Suddenly, the world opened up. She could choose almost any course that took her fancy.

Auntie Rae was more than excited. She was ecstatic. Robian told me she was an unusual sort of a lady, something of an eccentric, an academic and also an atheist whose god was the daily horoscope.

Suddenly she had plans for her young niece! Forget Teachers' College. Here was an opportunity to reach for the stars...

Auntie Rae was a very influential person in the family and she was pushing hard to have Robian accept the Commonwealth Scholarship offer. It was the last day to enrol – in fact the last hours, for Robian had three hours to make up her mind. She knew what she wanted: a career as a teacher. The young sixteen year-old was faced with three options: first, accept the Commonwealth Scholarship offer; second, accept the Teachers' College Scholarship offer and third; if the latter, what college to choose.

Auntie Rae applied the pressure as she faced growing resistance from her niece. Robian believed God was calling her to be a teacher.

Finally – and I suspect in some exasperation, Auntie Rae decided to consult the horoscope reading for that day, and abide by whatever it told her. Robian and her mother watched as Auntie Rae grabbed her favourite magazine and skipped through the pages until she found the daily horoscope. It read, almost word for word: 'Someone close to you has to make an important decision today. Do not interfere in the making of that decision.'

A stunned silence followed, and true to her word, Auntie Rae kept her peace as Robian chose, first... to go to Teachers' College and second, to go to Wagga Wagga Teachers' College, despite the fact that at that stage, her parents lived in Broken Hill, hundreds of miles to the north west.

'I graduated from Wagga Teachers' College,' Robian told me, 'and my first appointment was to Moulamein, in the state's south west; and who should be a teacher at a nearby school? None other than Ianrob, who was to become my husband, who in time was to become a student for the ministry, who six years after that, was to graduate with you, Lachlan.'

Truly, 'through each perplexing path of life,' God guides our wandering footsteps. How about you? Looking back on your life, can you see the work of the divine Presence? (While you're thinking about it, the fire has burned down far enough to think about slipping a slice of bread onto the toasting fork. I'll do one for you too... Hmm – is that hail or snow at the window?

Meg's Story

I've known Meg for many years. She's one of the finest people one could ever meet, as is her husband. She is not given to flights of fancy. She was in one of the church youth groups in one of my parishes. (I nearly said 'many years ago' but I don't think she would want me to say that – seems like yesterday anyway!)

This is an excerpt from a recent, personal letter that she's given me permission to relate to you. I asked her especially, for it is very beautiful:

'...Yes indeed Lachlan, I do believe many folk have indeed had some sort of inexplicable experience and many of us would love to know of ones that others have had. It only increases our faith. I know my own mother saw her deceased mother a few times over the days leading up to her own passing. Though I was by Mum's bedside at those times, I didn't see anything or experience personally the joy my mother felt. My mother just kept saying to me 'Mum's here and she looks so beautiful.' I shall never forget the joy and peace it brought to my mother as she lay in pain, dying of cancer. Was it the morphine speaking? I prefer to think it was a higher Power than morphine. My own experience happened without morphine or any other brain bender to blame, while sitting up in bed breastfeeding my youngest child during the night, when she was just a baby. Though the light was on and I saw nothing, and no one physical was there, there came a gentle sighing/breathing sound in the room with me, which went on for some time. I wasn't at all frightened, though I have never forgotten the sound, or the feeling that it was some female sighing over the sight of my babe in arms. The old couple who had built our first home were both deceased and childless, so I've always felt it could have been her there – or perhaps my wonderful own grandmother, whom a few members of our family believe to be some sort of guardian angel to us all. It is certainly my belief too. Have you had any folk mention the odd appearance of birds after a loved one passes? When my own lovely father died, my husband and I were in Dad's backyard when an owl flew down and sat on the rotary clothesline right next to where we were standing. Never in all their or my years of living there, had owls ever visited, let alone stopped so close to be part of our conversation for so long. Both of us were so taken aback by the close, friendly gentle nature of this owl and its determination to be with us, that we both joked that it was Dad come back to visit. Crazy I know..... but we both felt the same way, and since then I have overheard a few folk mentioning the strange presence of birds in similar circumstances. Now we have a glorious peacock visiting us at present. We don't know where he has come from, though he comes and goes as he chooses, but mostly stays very comfortably within earshot of where we are; either sprawled out on our verandahs or strutting around the gardens...'

Meg's parents were also members of that congregation and I will never forget them either, for they were like their children in so many ways, and in my mind, I can see them now... gracious and kindly, who played an active role in the congregation and were wonderful role models for all the younger ones in the church.

In regard to Meg's query regarding birds – the answer is yes, I have.

If I haven't told you already, ask me – but be careful. I have a regrettable habit of repeating myself. (Ask Janet. Ask Janet).

The Dorrigo Mountain Spider

There were giants in the earth in those days. Genesis 6:4a (AV).

The story I am about to relate to you has nothing to do with the supernatural or paranormal, but it fits well into *and other true stories* – and true it is, I can assure you.

It was told to me by the two people who saw the creature, and who at the time were no more than a few feet from it, fortunately viewed from within their car.

Anyway, let me tell you the story more or less as Brendan told it to me. By the way, Brendan S and his wife Jenny are highly respected business people within their community, related by marriage to some of our family members (but not to Janet or me). It's unimaginable to think that people of their calibre and standing would make up such a bizarre story, which, on the face of it, would bring them either fame or ridicule. It brought them neither, for they told few what they had seen, which to my mind is further evidence of truth. Brendan said that the year was somewhere in the early 80's; probably 1983.

Brendan and Jenny were heading east, down the Dorrigo Mountain Road very late one night – in fact it was really morning, for it was about 1.30am. They were returning from Gunnedah, Jenny's hometown, to their own home on the coast.

'It was a very dark night,' Brendan recalled, 'and there was a drizzle of rain. Our car was a fairly new Holden Statesman, which had powerful lights. As well, a pair of quartz-halogen driving lights was fitted, so the lights were very bright. On one section of the road, not far from the top and not far past a small off-road sightseeing platform, the lights picked up an object moving slowly across the road. In fact it was right at the end of the lights' range. I knew it could not be a small object, such as a rabbit, because I don't think I would have noticed it. To be on the safe side, I slowed down as I approached the object. As I drew closer and the lights revealed clearly and fully what it was, my mind found it hard to grasp what I was seeing. Still crossing slowly and apparently oblivious of my presence, was a giant spider – but a spider of such proportions that I really couldn't believe what I was seeing. My initial feeling was one of terror. I glanced at Jenny and noted that she was sleeping. By that time I had passed the spider, and still doubting the evidence of my eyes, turned the car around and drove back. The creature was still there, still moving slowly. I thought to myself, 'If I tell her about this when we get home, there is no way she is going to believe it,' so I woke her and told her to look. She looked – and was also terrified.

There is no way a spider should be so massive. At the time I knew virtually nothing about the spider family, but I did know I'd never heard of anything like it.

To give you some idea, try to imagine a spider the size of a wombat, or maybe a little smaller, or maybe a dog about that size. That's what we were looking at, just a few feet from us, fully revealed in the powerful lights of the car as well as the white glare of the quartz-halogen lights. I remember it was a solid spider, with powerful, hairy legs. It wasn't a spindly spider, such as a giant daddy long-legs!

We know exactly what we were looking at, and we know we can never forget it.

Since then, I've examined many photos of spiders to try to find something that bore some similarity, if not in size, then in shape, and from what I can see, the closest in appearance would have to be something like a bird-eating spider, which is I think is the largest species of spider in Australia, Even so, the spider we saw that night on the Dorrigo mountain road would have to be a hundred times larger.'

That story should have the world's natural scientists running around in circles, but it hasn't, simply because they've never heard it before. I heard the story from one of Jenny's relations quite a few years ago, but it was only recently that I spoke personally to Brendan and Jenny about it.

So, how do we account for such a creature that stands outside our understanding of what a spider should be? I have read that there have been unconfirmed sightings of giant spiders of roughly the size Brendan and Jenny saw, in the Congo and also somewhere in South America. There is then some possible precedent for such a large spider. I have no intention whatsoever of trying to explain away or rationalise what Brendan and Jenny saw. I believe them completely, and always have. Some sceptics of course have said that the couple may have seen something like a wombat, but if you've been listening to what I just told you, that suggestion is impossible. Others have suggested that it could not have been an arachnid (spider) because apparently spiders don't have lungs, and any spider growing to such a size would die because it would not have the capacity to breathe. That suggestion stands outside my knowledge of the arachnid species. As I have said, I am not trying to give any technical explanations for anything I've been telling you because I would be speaking out of my own ignorance. All I can say is that if what I was told about an arachnid's lack of lungs, then maybe it was of the arachnid family but had other attributes, such as lungs.

Anyway, let's get off this natural history thing and turn to something I know at least a little about. Let's take a look at that text I quoted above from Genesis 6:4a.

If you turn to your Bible when you get home, you'll probably look in vain for the word 'giants' in that passage, unless your preference is the King James (Authorised) Version. The word the modern translations use in place of 'giants' is Nephilim' with a capital 'N.' That's because the passage reads on to indicate that the giants belonged to a race separate from ordinary humans, which the more modern translations indicate. The letters 'im' on the end of a Hebrew word generally indicate a plural; for instance cherub (singular) and cherubim (plural).

The interesting thing for us, however, is the fact that the word 'nephelim' or in English, 'giants' was not restricted to a race of men.

It could also refer to other creatures; monsters no less, and we certainly know they existed, in forms of dinosaurs and other massive creatures. (None of these is mentioned in recognisable detail in the Bible).

Australia is an ancient land, cut off for millennia from the rest of the world. Creatures exist in this country that have no equivalent anywhere else on earth, such as the platypus.

If you know the Dorrigo state forest, you'll know that it's massive in size, and is also dense. Who knows what's down there? It's only recently that a variety of trees, millions of years old, was discovered in another part of NSW; the Wollemi pines, now in many a garden, but they can be huge.

What if some species of spider survived down the ages and still lives its secretive life in some hidden area of the Dorrigo state forest?

I think I mentioned that in 1966 I had a very nasty accident when

... and other true stories

serving in the parish of Dorrigo. I missed an S-bend on that same Dorrigo Mountain Road, not too far from where Brendan and Jenny saw the spider. I was on my way to Bellingen to take a church service there one Sunday evening. My little Morris Major fell two hundred feet. My survival was a miracle. Had I even suspected there were spiders the size of wombats down there, I'd have run up that two hundred feet, without even pausing.

There is another text in the Bible referring to a giant, terrifying creature, which the writer of Job refers to as Leviathan. To me, it sounds as if it may be a crocodile, or similar creature:.

On earth there is not his like. Job 41:33. From the King James version of the Bible).

That, for me, sums up the giant spider of Dorrigo Mountain.

The life beyond this life

12

The Final Chapter

When I speak of the 'final chapter' I am not talking about the final chapter of this story, but rather the final chapter of our earthly life.

We all know that our life will end one day; in fact the life of every living earthly thing finally comes to a close. Jesus once said, *Heaven and earth will pass away, but My words will never pass away.* Matthew 24:35.

We know that He was talking about the physical earth and heavens; not the spiritual heaven, for He made it plain that life itself can be eternal.

Vera Ryan, in her letter,, remarked on a quote from Kerry Packer, the newspaper magnate, who 'died' briefly but was revived. He is reported to have said, 'I've been on the other side, and let me tell you, there's nothing there.'

Others contradict that view, as Vera made plain.

Pre-1492, a Spanish coin had an outline of the known world and the words, 'Ne Plus Altra' (Nothing Beyond). Then Christopher Columbus returned from his historic voyage and the word 'Ne' (Nothing) on the coin was dropped, which altered the meaning to: 'More Beyond.'

For many today, any thought of life beyond this life is meaningless, and with Kerry Packer they believe there is 'Nothing beyond.' Death is final. 'Once yer dead, yer dead,' as someone once said to me. People may believe that before death, but they certainly won't believe it after they cross 'the great divide.'

'Way back when I must have been a teenager, there was a newspaper report of someone who was pronounced dead but was miraculously resuscitated; who described the experience as 'like a beautiful dream.' That incident occurred quite a few years before medical science had made considerable advances, and doctors began to resuscitate many who were initially pronounced dead. Since then, many remarkable books have been written, frequently by medical people, such as *Life after Life* by the famous Dr Raymond Moody, and a reasonably new book by another medical practitioner, the noted radiation oncologist Dr Jeffrey Long: *Evidence of the Afterlife*. Those and other books contain amazing stories. 'Time' magazine dated 22 January 2010 reports an interview by Laura Fitzpatrick with Dr Long. When asked if there was evidence of life after death, Dr Long replied, 'If you look at the scientific evidence, the answer is an unequivocal yes.'

Dr Long is more than happy to take on the sceptics. He says however that when a person is permanently dead and can't be revived at all, that's when faith steps in.

It's not unusual these days to read of people who, while experiencing brief clinical death, have returned with amazing stories of rising from their earthly bodies, to look down on the doctors working feverishly to save them. Usually there is a great degree of similarity in the stories.

To this day many believe that those experiences are simply the effects of dying brain cells starved of oxygen. It is claimed that pilots undergoing extreme G-forces have the same experiences when their brains become starved of oxygen, which is doubtless true, but new studies reveal important differences. For instance, there are many reports of people, clinically dead at the time, who gave accurate descriptions of people and accurate reports of conversations in other rooms when they had no way of knowing, apart from being there. All say they could look down from above on the scene below.

I am going to tell you some stories of people I know, who have been kind enough to tell me of their experience while clinically, if briefly dead, and are prepared to allow me to pass them on.

Stan's Story

Stan and I have been friends for many years, for we met while serving at the Army Aviation Centre in Oakey Qld. He was a RAEME major and I was the Base padre.

Stan was aged seventeen at the time of his 'Near Death Experience' or as they are termed, NDE.

He told me that at age seventeen, he was invincible – he thought. He had a nippy Morris Minor 1000 and drove it to the limit (not something unknown among seventeen year-olds, as the statistics, which include myself at the same age, sadly testify).

One evening he and a friend headed back to his unit at Bandiana, on the Victorian side of Albury, after a night out. They were in Stan's Morris and he was low-flying in his usual fashion, which we can describe euphemistically as 'enthusiastic.'

There's a small bridge before one reaches the big bridge that spans the Murray River into Victoria, and there was a fog that night.

From what Stan told me, I don't think the fog and the hidden bridge deterred his driving speed in the slightest – when suddenly out of the fog he saw the bridge, and the car was heading straight for it. He swung the wheel hard right, but the back bumper bar clipped a white post and the vehicle spun into the bridge. Somehow, Stan's head must have come into violent contact with something very solid in the car (no seat belts in those days) and he sustained a severe head injury.

He doesn't remember anything much after that. Later, he learned that his friend sustained a broken shoulder.

He was unconscious when the ambulance crew pulled him from the car and took him to hospital. He was unconscious and probably clinically dead, when he found himself leaving his body, floating towards the ceiling. From there he looked down on the three doctors who were fighting to save his life. Stan also said there was a minister or priest; a clergyman in there with them at the time. (I suspect he was probably one who had been called in for the Last Rites). No one else mentioned the clergyman, but Stan saw him distinctly.

Stan has a distinct memory of a very bright light, into which he felt himself being inexorably drawn...

His next memory was waking up in a bed in Wodonga Hospital.

In time he went on to complete his career in the Army, which included a year in Vietnam, before retiring with the rank of Major.

Like the rest of my friends whom I've kept from my time in the Army, Stan is a no-nonsense, practical man who is incapable of devising such a story. If he said that's what happened, I know without a shadow of doubt, that's what happened.

Now here is another part of the story with a strange connection.

Stan's mother was a particularly fine lady whom I knew quite well. She lived to a good age and, like her sons, was as honest as the day. When she died, I had the privilege of officiating at her funeral.

When Stan had his accident, his mother didn't know at the time because she was away from her home and unable to be contacted. In fact she was visiting a friend of hers who was psychic. Her friend had a message for her. She told her that someone close to her was in hospital, but she didn't know the name. She could see, she said, a building with a large red cross on the roof, and described it.

Not long after, Stan's mother was advised of the accident and rushed to Wodonga to be with her son. She told him that as the car approached Wodonga hospital, it was exactly as her psychic friend had described it, with the Red Cross emblem on the roof.

Marilyn's story: The day I died

As told by MW

Being from a different cultural background from Christian society, I have often tried to make sense of the events that happened in April 1973. I still remember the event very clearly to this day.

I was living about 40 kilometres from a small town in north-west

NSW. At the time our family of three girls, ranging in age from five years to three months old, lived in a caravan on a property where my husband worked as a mechanic.

Late one Friday afternoon, I began to feel very unwell. As an asthmatic I have always been conscious of anything that makes breathing difficult for me. I struggled through with my medication, which seemed to ease it for a while.

By Saturday morning I was worse, and by the afternoon I was finding it hard to breathe. My husband stayed with the children, while a son of the property-owner drove me to another town to see a doctor, who gave me an injection to assist my breathing. That seemed to work for a short while, but on the way home I became violently ill. Nothing like it had ever happened to me before. I'd had the injections previously and they had always relieved the breathing and distress.

I returned to the caravan around 7.30pm and it seemed to settle. It was getting toward the cooler part of the year, and the van needed to be warmed, especially for the children, but it was detrimental for me.

I continually asked my husband to reduce the heat and take the blankets off me. He kept repeating, 'You are sick and need to keep warm.'

'No,' I insisted, 'I need to have air coming into the van. I need air!'

From about 2.00 am on Sunday I began to feel frightened and pleaded with my husband to take me to hospital, but he told me to stay calm. 'We can't get the kids out yet,' he told me, 'it's too cold.'

Finally, around 5.00am, we left for the hospital.

At the hospital entrance one of the doctors saw me in the car just as she was leaving, and called the night supervisor.

At that point all I remember is being assisted from the car into a wheelchair, as the Doctor shouted directions at the staff.

I think at that time, knowing I was now in safe hands, I seemed just to let go. From that point, for several days, I remember nothing of the outside world. I do know that at some point I died.

I remember very clearly travelling through a tunnel with a beautiful white light. Not bright – and yet it was, with no glare. So, so peaceful, like being on a cloud. How long I travelled I do not know.

As I came to the end of the tunnel I saw a lady standing there, whom I recognised as my mother. She had died when I was three years old, so I really did not know or have any life memories of her at all. I'd seen photos of her and I recognised her.

She stood beside a man who had a long white beard, who wore a long white gown, and had a walking stick in his right hand. In the area behind them stood other people, but I could not clearly identify any faces. The whole area was as though I was in the midst of a cloud.

As she stood beside the man with the cane, she kept pushing her hand toward me as if to say 'go back, go back.' I seemed to hover just on the edge of the tunnel. Suddenly it seemed as if a very strong vacuum pulled me back along the tunnel. I wanted to stay! I wanted to see my mother!

Several days later, when I awoke from the coma, I found I was in an oxygen tent, used to treat collapsed lungs.

One of the nursing sisters who had been 'specialling' me on a 24-hour basis asked casually, 'Well what do the pearly gates look like?'

At that time I had absolutely no idea what she meant and I didn't for some time.

After a week or so, when I was well enough to have some time out of the tent, I took my chart and read it. Yes - I had actually died. My blood pressure was 50 over nothing!

Now I understood what the Sister had meant.

Despite the fact that many try to explain away my experience and similar experiences others have had ('lack of oxygen to the brain' etc.) the fact remains: I know it was real and it happened to me.'

Thank you for that intriguing account Marilyn, (good friend and former neighbour) of an experience that can't be explained away by simple theories, much as many would like to. Your story is another reminder to us all that there is life beyond this life, as evidenced over and over.

A friend, a minister, told me that when he was at school, a girl in his class aged about 10 years, had a severe heart attack, and 'died' on the operating table. She told him that as she lay there, she left her body and floated above it, from where she could see the doctors working as they tried desperately to save her, before suddenly finding herself back in her body. She never forgot the odd sensation. That was long before the 'Life after Death' experiences were given wide publicity, and she was only ten anyway.

When my friend left school, he lost track of her. He became a schoolteacher, then a minister.

Years later, he became a lecturer at a theological college, where he met her again. He was delighted to learn that her health was good. She had married a fine man and they were engaged in Christian mission work among the Indigenous people in the Northern Territory.

Hamish's Story

My friend Hamish never knew what hit him on that fateful day some years ago.

He can recall going off to fetch coffee for one of his colleagues, and also his colleague's words: 'Don't forget I take milk in mine!' Almost everything about that day is still shrouded in oblivion and some vague recollections, apart from what he was told later.

His young son found him lying on the floor of the family room of their home, realised his father was comatose, and rushed off to fetch his mother. Hamish said he was dimly aware of his son's presence, but after that slipped back into unconsciousness again.

When his family found him, he was no longer in the family room but lying face-down in the grass beside his car, again comatose, with the car keys in his hand.

At some time he recalled an experience of falling UP, in a huge 'fluorescent tunnel' as he described it. It was the only way he felt he could describe the brightness of his surroundings, and the experience. At the end of the tunnel Hamish could see what appeared to be a cross, or a person with outstretched arms, or a very bright light – even brighter than the one along which he was travelling. 'I can't explain it,' he told me; 'the light ahead was even brighter than the walls of the tunnel, but it did not hurt my eyes.'

He was very dimly aware of a voice coming from somewhere – a human voice he knew, calling: 'Don't go! Come back!'

Later he would discover that the voice was Maria's, the wife of one of his friends, who with the others had found him lying beside his car.

Now, however, he had moved on from her voice and was looking down from a great height: 'looking down on creation' was Hamish's description. From there he could look down on those who were running to help. The ambulance had been called, as well as the doctor and a nurse, and from his lofty height he could see them as they ran to him. He could accurately describe the position of each car, and the location of the ambulance.

Later, those who had run to help were astounded as Hamish described accurately the direction from which each had come.

A series of tests followed, such as squeezing his ear lobes and pressing sharp objects into the soles of his feet, looking for signs of life. Then he heard the nurse say, 'He's already dead.' He knew then that physically he showed no signs of life.

He was loaded into the ambulance and as it drove off, he heard the volunteer ambulance officer say to the ambulance driver, 'No need to hurry – he's already gone.' The nurse was also in the ambulance with Hamish at the time.

There were other incidents along the way, but finally he was in the ICU at Dubbo Base Hospital, where further tests were carried out and the 'Packer Whackers' applied, all of which finally helped save his life.

There are some mysteries still attached to the story that will never be known; such as: how did he get to his car from the living-room floor of his house? It can only be assumed that he had some form of temporary improvement, and went to get help for himself, for his car keys were in his hand.

Hamish was to discover that he'd had a massive stroke, which has affected him slightly in one way and another to this day. The good news, however, is that he has retained full use of heart and mind and limbs, with no paralysis at all. He has been a useful servant of the Lord for many years now, serving Him right well. Outwardly, there is no sign that he'd ever been affected by the stroke.

I've known Hamish for some years, and, like others I know who have been through a similar experience, he tells me that he no longer has the slightest fear of dying. He went to the edge, liked what he saw, and would have been happy to keep going. The Lord, however, still has work for him to do. His 'crown of righteousness' is still some way ahead!

Greg's Story

I know Greg quite well. He and his family live in a country town in

NSW and are staunch members of their church, where Greg does some lay preaching as required. Again, any stories that I repeat are from people I know and trust, and Greg and his family are certainly in that league. What Greg told me is a detailed account of something very unpleasant that happened to him during his time in the Army.

In 1984 Greg, whose corps was RAE (Royal Australian Engineers) was on exercise with his unit, 18 Field Squadron in the High Range training area, out of Townsville Qld. The unit was building a medium girder bridge – 'bridging the gap' is the term the engineers use, Greg told me.

Greg was at the extension end, working under the bridge, when one of the pins holding the railing sheared off, and the railing, weighing approximately eight kilos, let go. The railing fell over a metre and a half, striking Greg on the head.

He had no recollection of anything that followed for some time. He woke up in hospital, where he remained for some days until he was declared fit, and returned to his unit.

Some time later, he kept having black-outs, or 'fainting spells' as they were called, which the doctors decided finally were heat-related, and he was posted to 17 Construction Squadron at Holsworthy NSW.

From there he was posted to the Recruit Training Base at Kapooka, just out of Wagga Wagga NSW, where the WRAAC School had just been posted, from Middle Head NSW. Greg and others set to work, building the WRAAC School Q-store. (WRAAC: Women's Royal Australian Army Corps).

The medical opinion that Greg's condition was heat-related was proved to be in error when around December 1985, Greg's sudden collapses returned, together with seizures that had the medicos convinced that he was an epileptic. For some reason, it appears that no one to that date considered the possibility that his condition could have been related to the blow on the head.

After spending more time in hospital; this time in the military hospital at Ingleburn NSW, where he underwent further tests, Greg received a posting order to the Dog Squad, which was quickly rescinded because of his seizures.

The almost inevitable Med Board followed and Greg found himself medically discharged from the Australian Army.

He took himself back to his hometown in country NSW where he settled down with his wife into that very pleasant community, unaware of what was to follow. He was still suffering seizures, still trying to get his medication under control.

One morning it happened. Greg was in the shower when he suffered a massive seizure and fell. Fortunately his wife heard him fall and immediately called the doctor and the ambulance. The doctor was the first to arrive and recognised that Greg was hovering on the edge of death. He plunged a syringe of whatever doctors fancy into his heart, then accompanied Greg in the ambulance to Dubbo Base Hospital.

From there the Air Ambulance took him to Royal Prince Alfred hospital in Sydney. Somewhere between Sydney Airport and RPA, Greg suffered another seizure, and died. Upon arrival at the hospital he was pronounced 'DOA' – dead on arrival.

Greg's next memory is of himself in the hospital corridor, looking down on his earthly body from above, surrounded by a white light of indescribable brilliance. He had no fear – in fact he felt himself caught up in a sensation of peace and calm and serenity that defies earthly description.

'It's impossible to describe to anyone who has never experienced it personally,' Greg said.

The emergency team at RPA was able to revive Greg within minutes of his 'death.' His recovery was slow but sure, but finally he was released to his grateful family and friends back in his hometown.

There is a very happy sequel to this story. Since returning home, Greg's recovery has been more than complete. What do I mean by that? I hear you ask. Well, virtually from the time Greg returned to his hometown, he has never suffered another 'fainting attack' or 'black-out' and he has never suffered another so-called 'epileptic' attack. He enjoys perfect health and is on no medication; in fact he has a licence entitling him to drive buses.

He is quite content, living in peace and contentment with his wife and family, taking part in the life of his church and other activities in the community.

'One thing I do know,' Greg told me, 'is that I now have no fear of dying. If it had been my time to die permanently, I would have been quite content, and even eager, to see what God had prepared for me in the life to come.'

As I listened to Greg, the words of an old hymn floated into my mind. It's one from the old Presbyterian hymn book and I'm sure it can be found in many another hymn book too. It's called 'Children of the Heavenly King' and the words are by John Cennick.

It was written a time when infant mortality rates were very high, for there were no antibiotics, no life-saving serum to inject into the heart, no highly advanced medicines or life-saving drugs. Two of the lines of the hymn go:

Lord, obediently we go,
Gladly leaving all below…

I think that is the way most who have stood at the portals of the Great Beyond have felt, before being returned to their mortal bodies. All whom I've spoken to have indicated that same sensation.

Cennick himself died young, for he was only 37 when he was called to his eternal home in 1755. I'm sure he felt that same eagerness, despite his young age: 'Gladly leaving all below.'

Alora, the swan

Hmmm – as I reflect on the stories of those who have had a tantalising glimpse of the other side of this life, I think I'll have to fortify myself with a cocoa brew, and give the fire a stir with the poker, but before I do so, I feel I'll have to mention Alora.

The following happened to me, and not so long ago; in fact it would have been about fifteen years ago. I could find it in my diary of that year if I was sure just what year and month it was. I know it's in there ...

Anyway, in view of the fact that others have told their stories and have been prepared to face scepticism and even ridicule, much as some fear it, I think I should be prepared to do the same and face the same possibility. There is some wisdom in the old adage: 'It's better to remain silent and let people think you are an idiot, than to open your mouth and prove it beyond doubt.' Well, this idiot is about to speak of an incident that took place one night, and again it was at the Manly manse, where many unusual incidents took place, as I related earlier.

Once again, at the risk of boring you witless, I must repeat that I have never sought the experience that happened that night or any other; it just happened one evening when I retired. I suppose I was asleep, or in a trance-state I can't say. I sometimes wonder whether I had actually died, in a sense, for it was not like a dream. Dreams have qualities of their own, as do visions. I cannot remember any dream I've had, ever, but on the occasions when what has occurred has been more like a vision, or a visitation; well, that's different. I remember them vividly. I'd be surprised if I'm not speaking for almost all those who have had that sort of experience. There is an unmistakable difference in ordinary dreams, dreams in the biblical sense, and visions or visitations. Another reason that I've been reluctant to talk about this one, is the fact that I don't quite know in what category to put it. I suppose I'd better just blurt it out and let you make up your mind. I've been babbling on for the last few minutes because of my reluctance to impart this story.

As I said, I went to bed, and somewhere in the 'wee sma' hours' as my dear old Scottish Granny used to say, I found myself somewhere, and before me was a swan... a black swan, exquisitely beautiful, seemingly unaware of my presence, in a pond surrounded by rushes.

Behind me, from somewhere, a voice was speaking, telling me the story of Alora, the swan. What I will never forget, or ever want to forget, is the voice. I think it must have been the voice of God, or perhaps some heavenly being, telling me the story, for the voice was full of beauty and love; an ethereal quality that was so... well, I can't describe it. It was a male voice, that I do remember. The swan's name was mentioned as the beautiful story unfolded. I never wanted to leave wherever I was. Part of me - spirit, soul, was somewhere where my earthly body was not. I suppose it was snoring comfortably in the main bedroom of the manse.

Had I been given the choice of going or staying, I would have stayed. I never wanted to leave... and that seems to tell me that the essential quality that makes me me; my soul or spirit, was not where it normally resides, within this generously proportioned frame. That is the only way I can describe it. I can never forget Alora, and I can never forget that heavenly (in the sense of belonging to heaven) voice, which told the story of the swan with such divine tenderness. Sadly, what I can't remember is the story; only that it was a beautiful, unearthly - the sort of unearthliness that speaks or sings of heaven itself. Perhaps I wasn't meant to remember.

In his lovely book *The Wind in the Willows*, Kenneth Grahame recounts how Ratty and Mole hear a song that the wind is whispering to the reeds by the river bank: *Lest limbs be reddened and rent, I spring the trap that is set... Strays I find in it, wounds I bind in it..* but surely you will forget... and the reeds sigh, *forget, forget...*(From the chapter, 'The Piper at the Gates of Dawn'). Ever since, I've tried to analyse the meaning of my dream/vision. When God speaks to us, it's usually for a reason, as Moses discovered when he stopped to watch a bush in the desert that burst mysteriously into flame, or as Paul discovered when thrown to the ground that day on the Damascus Road.

Neither of them expected God to intrude so suddenly into their lives.

I sometimes wonder if the divine message that night was sent to allay my doubts and fears concerning the animal kingdom, and to reassure me that the beautiful creatures I've especially loved over the years; my four-footed companions, are indeed in heaven... Possibly. I can't really say.

'A Glimpse of Eternity'

The amazing story I'm about to recount here takes us beyond the immediate experience of clinical death, as related by Stan, Marilyn, Hamish and Greg, to a much deeper (or higher, really) level. Ian McCormack went beyond the apparent first stage of death: the light and the tunnel, to the next, after which there is no return. If you read this story and believe it, as I do, it will call you to consider very carefully where you want to spend eternity; in heaven or hell.

Anyway, 'A glimpse of Eternity' is the title of a small booklet in my possession. The story I am about to relate concerning the subject of the book is nothing less than astounding. Until recently I had never met Ian McCormack, apart from contact with him via quite a lot via emails. He now lives in the UK, in London, but was born and raised in New Zealand.

I first heard of Ian when someone gave me a DVD called The Lazarus Phenomenon.

It's a Christian DVD; re-enactments that tell the true stories of two men who 'died' and were resuscitated. The first is the story of a black African pastor, who died briefly after a car accident. His story is amazing enough. I think Ian's is even more so, although there are great similarities in the two accounts. As soon as I saw Ian's story, and listened to him, I had an overwhelming sensation that I was listening to the truth, told by a godly man who was full of the Holy Spirit. That sensation (it's more than 'sensation,' but it's about the only way I can describe it in understandable terms) was not much different from the Call I had, when I knew God was calling me into the ministry of the Church. I was, and am, completely convinced of the authenticity of Ian's account.

Ian was pronounced dead for fifteen to twenty minutes after being stung five times by deadly box jellyfish while diving off the coast of Mauritius. Any one of the stings should have killed him. The toxin from the box jellyfish is believed to be the second deadliest poison known to man. (I don't know what is the deadliest, but pens and tongues can rate high on the list).

At the time, Ian was an atheist, seeking an 'endless summer:' diving, surfing, travelling, a life with very slack moral boundaries, despite the fact that he was raised in a Christian home and had loving parents. Ian's mother is a devout Christian. His parents gave him every opportunity in life that a reasonably affluent couple (both school teachers) could afford to give their children: a loving family, lots of holidays and a good education, including university. He graduated with a degree in Agriculture from Lincoln University and spent the first two years of his working life as a consultant for the NZ Dairy Board.

After that, he decided that it was time for him to see the world; what the New Zealanders refer to as 'the OE' (Overseas Experience). He set off, following the endless summer, unaware of what lay in store for him. His journeying took him to many places: Australia, Europe and Asia, and as a non-believer, he tried most things that a life without God or moral constraints is prepared to try. Ian loved the outdoors and in Australia developed a love of surfing. His adventures took him to the island of Mauritius off the east coast of Africa, where he lived for a time with a local native family. They took him snorkelling, where he learned to catch crayfish and crabs for the family table. It was on a night dive that it happened. He swam into a school of box jellyfish and was stung a total of five times. One sting can - and without medical aid frequently does, kill. At least sixty people have been known to die from the effects of box jellyfish stings in northern Australian coastal waters. The box jellyfish off Mauritius certainly killed Ian; a fact that the medical staff at the hospital confirmed, but it was during that temporary sleep of death that heaven was revealed – as well as hell. His death experience and recovery through God's grace and forgiveness resulted in a transformation from the death of the soul to life in the Spirit. Before he was totally free from the old life, however, he had a couple of dark experiences as the past sought to reclaim him, which I found quite frightening, even to read of them.

In the prologue I mentioned the Arabic word *gūl*, which the Concise Oxford Dictionary translates as a 'protean desert demon.' As a reminder of what I said earlier, the word 'protean' means that it is able to assume many forms. There is no doubt in my mind that the spirits and demons of the ancient past haven't looked at the modern world with all its technology and vast numbers of world-weary citizens who don't appear to believe in anything much, and said, 'Aw, no one believes in us anymore. I'm going home.' Whatever was the thing in human guise that tried to reclaim Ian, I hope and pray it never visits me, enticing as it may make itself. I'll be praying some of the words of William Cowper's beautiful hymn, *O For A Closer Walk With God*, one verse of which goes:

The dearest idol I have known,
Whate'r that idol be,
Help me to tear it from its throne
And worship only Thee.

Ian's description of heaven is breathtakingly beautiful, although he says that nothing can do it justice. He was also shown hell; a place so terrifying that he has made it his life's mission to try to convince people of its reality, with its tormented souls and its satanic creatures. The mission Jesus calls him to do is to lead people to faith in Him and to embrace life in the Spirit, while they have time.

Ian now has a lovely wife and family, is an ordained minister and is involved in his own mission work, together with his family. He is not wealthy. He refused money from me on the grounds that he can't sell what God has given him.

He has written a small book (eighty pages) of his experience, including his life before and after, (as told by Jenny Sharkey), with several photos. He sent me a copy, gratis. By the way, if you have an internet connection, you can Google Ian and his story, simply by typing in Ian McCormack, but make sure you select the correct Ian McCormack, for there are several others of that name.

Ian has told me that a full film of his story is to be released, probably about October 2013 and its title is THE PERFECT WAVE. Keep an eye out for it.

I've read other books of those who have died for a time and have gone beyond being drawn towards the light, who tell astonishing stories. One, for instance, is *90 Minutes in Heaven*, which is the story of a Baptist pastor, Don Piper, who was dead for ninety minutes, after being involved in an horrific car accident: 'A true story of death and life' as it is described. Another is the account of a little boy, Colton Burpo, the son of a pastor, who also died for a time. Weeks later, back at his home, the boy began to speak of heavenly things that a small boy would have heard nothing about, despite the fact that his father was a pastor. When little Colton saw a photo of his deceased grandfather, he identified him at once as one he'd seen in heaven. The boy's father, when he recognised the fact that Colton was speaking of things he'd seen during the brief time of his physical death, which at his age the father knew he could not possibly have learned otherwise, began to write down his son's experiences and eventually it became a best-selling book: *Heaven is for Real* as told by his father, Todd Burpo with Lynn Vincent. The book has photos of the young boy and his family and also details of how to get in touch. (Both that book and *90 Minutes in Heaven* are available from Koorong Books, the Christian book shop with outlets all over Australia).

Inevitably those stories, and Ian's, evoke comment, not all of it favourable, from those who have various criticisms. Some point out for instance, the words of scripture: *It is destined for man to die once.* (Hebrews 9:27). Off the top of my head I can think of at least two instances where Jesus raised people from the dead: Jairus's daughter (Luke 8:49-55), and Jesus' friend Lazarus, (John 11:38-44). I am certain that the writer of the Letter to the Hebrews was referring to permanent death; the death of those who are beyond resuscitation. Only the Lord of life can resuscitate them. Lazarus, for instance, was dead for days, and decomposition had commenced. In the above two instances, a time would come when they would die permanently, and be buried.

Jesus fulfilled the signs of the expected Messiah: *The blind receive sight, the lame walk, those who have leprosy are cured, the deaf hear, the dead are raised and the good news is preached to the poor.* Luke 7:22-23).

10 February 2013

Ian McCormack arrived in Brisbane and was in Sydney from 6-10 February. Janet and I and various family members and friends – as well as a vast congregation of other people – went to hear Ian, who was the guest speaker at Oxford Falls C3 Church. I listened to this man, who told his story and delivered his Christian message with a passion and commitment I could only dream about, and he made me quietly aware of my own shortcomings as a preacher. (He would have been dismayed to learn that, I think. He thinks well of everyone). He was amazing to listen to. Even after nearly thirty years since his brief experience of death and then being revived, he could not keep the emotion from his voice. It was not contrived. I was also delighted to observe that he has a great sense of Down Under style of humour to go with it! On the other hand, his story of heaven and the way he describes what happened, defy description. That was the fastest hour I've ever spent. If lives weren't touched that day, I'd be surprised.

Later, I went to see him, for he had some books and disks for me that I'd pre-ordered. The meeting was necessarily brief, for he was about to be whisked away to something else – a good hot cuppa I hope, and a rest, for the travel, followed by days and evenings of preaching and recounting his story must have been utterly draining. He is a good man. He sells the books and DVDs for cost, and the DVD has on it, 'Feel free to copy this DVD.' All he wants to do is get the message across. I watched the DVD. It has on it, first, his message as he tells it to an Australian audience somewhere and second, the re-enactment of the box jellyfish story.

He sells the disks for one dollar each. He feels he can't sell for profit what the Lord has given him. Of course there are many who will ridicule everything I've talked about in this yarn tonight. I'm expecting a great deal of scorn to be heaped on my head, but I don't mind at all, for I've certainly made myself very vulnerable. In fact I can well understand how unworldly, unreal and even false much of this may seem to many who have not experienced anything supernatural (apart possibly from religious belief) in their lives, while the response of others, I hope and pray, will be more positive. The general response may well be divided, like the response of the Athenians when Paul preached about Jesus to them at the Areopagus: *When they heard about the resurrection of the dead, some of them sneered, but others said, 'We want to hear you again on this subject.'* (Acts 17:32). All I can respond is that I am speaking the truth and I believe all the people I've been in contact with, are also speaking the truth; otherwise their stories would not be here. In time 'all will be revealed,' and I'm telling you now – it won't be 'ercule Poirot or Miss Marple who'll be doing the revealing!

The fact that both those books I mentioned a short time ago became best sellers, and that Ian McCormack has speaking engagements all over the world, should convince any thinking person of the deep yearning within the human spirit for our true home; to be with our Creator God, in heaven. The thirteen autobiographical books that St Augustine wrote towards the end of the fourth century AD came to be known as *The Confessions of St Augustine*. In Book 1, Augustine wrote: *You move us to delight in praising You; for You have formed us for Yourself, and our hearts are restless till they find rest in You.*

Augustine was raised in a Christian home of wealthy and devout parents. He too 'threw over the traces' at university, became a profligate and non-believer – until God took him in hand. He came under the influence of Ambrose, a Bishop of the Early Church, and under his guidance became one of the great champions of the Christian faith.

... *And that is the end of my story.* (Last line of a schoolboy parody that I once used to recite of Charles Wolfe's sombre and beautiful poem, 'Burial of Sir John Moore at Corunna').

I'm going to finish here. If you haven't fallen asleep by now, you're an insomniac.

I hope you've been given something to think about. If not, *then dispose of this container thoughtfully*; a message I'm seeing on more and more containers these days. This evening with you is a container of what I believe are remarkable and true stories. I hope it's to your taste. I hope it has given you something to think about, very deeply.

The Lord bless you and keep you, and may His face shine upon you, and be gracious unto you; The Lord lift up His countenance upon you and give you peace, this day, and always.

AMEN. AMEN. AMEN.

Epilogue

13

Oh well, the fire has died down to the stage where I would have to spend some time getting it up to its cheery state again, and to be honest, having spent the past couple of hours just talking to your attentive (I hope) ear, I'm almost hoarse. You've been such a patient listener, but just then I thought I detected the tiniest hint of a snore. It's almost time to call it a night. I'll be interested to learn your thoughts tomorrow about some of those strange and/or fascinating incidents I've mentioned.

Most of the stories I've told you tonight have been gleaned from my memory and from those of friends and family, and from some others. St John, in the concluding lines of his gospel wrote: *Now, there are many other things that Jesus did. If they were all written down one by one, I suppose that the whole world could not hold the books that would be written.* John 21:25.

We could apply the great Apostle's thoughts to the experiences countless numbers of people have had, concerning the mysterious world around us.

Talking can have a soporific effect on listeners – and not only listeners. A couple of weeks ago, in the middle of a sermon, I almost put myself to sleep... What? Oh, yeah, yeah, I remember that jibe someone made about clergy being employed in hospitals as anaesthetists – very amusing, I'm sure! It can be so funny, however, watching one's congregation from the pulpit. I remember one lady who used to bustle in, apparently full of life and energy. She liked to sit in the very front pew and gaze up at me, or whoever was preaching, her face alive with interest and anticipation. Every Sunday, within half an hour of the commencement of the service, she was unconscious, head on chest. Once, I noted a movement of an arm that indicated she was trying to pull a blanket over her head. At least it wasn't a pillow. I must say it was a trifle off-putting. Another lady 'way up the back of the Church used to yawn without covering her mouth, so from time to time during sermons I'd see something resembling a dark cave appear briefly... but there I go, rambling on again, well off the beaten track, which I promised not to do but did, here and there. It's an occupational hazard endured by those who sit in pews while listening to preachers.

As I think back on what I've said, that promise seems to have about as much substance as some of those delivered with apparent sincerity by some of our politicians. All the same, I've really enjoyed our fireside evening. Every now and then it's occurred to me that one day I should gather up all these memories and letters, and put them in a book. I wonder what I'd call it?

Nothing much comes to mind right now, but I think it would have to be along the lines of

The Ness Fireside Book of God Ghosts Ghouls and other true stories. What do you think? Anyway, keep your eye out for it. After all, you're in it.

... and other true stories

Index of stories

... and other true stories

1 GHOSTS — 8

The ghost of old 'Fortuna'	9
The ghost in Croydon house, London	12
The ghost in the mausoleum	13
The ghost who used 'Dencorub'	14
The mischievous ghost in the manse	15
The mysterious ghost at Kanwal	16
The girl in the chequered shirt	18
The ghost in the caravan	19
The ghost at the dressing table mirror	20
A ghost story from Canada	21
The ghost nurse of old 'Southall'	22
A ghostly warning	24
The swaggie ghost of Gravesend	28
Ghostly hands	29
The hair-pulling ghost in old London town	30

2 HAUNTINGS — 32

The haunted farm house	33
Haunted railway stations	36
Haunted railway tunnels	37
The haunted castle	39
The strange residents of Rocky hospital	41
Ghostly footsteps in old RPA	44

3 VISITATIONS — 46

A mother's visit from beyond the grave	47
The boy who returned to reassure his mother	48
A grandfather's reassurance	49
A mother brings peace from beyond	49

A message from Nan	52
A story from Thailand	52
The brother who came to say goodbye	53

4 UNEXPLAINABLE, INEXPLICABLE — 55

'You'll never take me alive'	56
The leaving of 'Taradale'	56
'I saw a man who wasn't there'	58
The clock that stopped when it shouldn't have	59
The clock that started when it shouldn't have	59
Merle's story	61
The piano that moved	62
Gallipoli 1990: did God have a hand in it?	66

5 PREMONITIONS — 72

A few thoughts	73
A premonition of an accident	75
The cowled lady	79
Heather's premonition	84
Joan's premonition	85
A wife's premonition	86
George's story	88
'If only'	90
'Duck, Nils!'	93
'I can hear the drums, Papa!'	97

6 'LET THE CHILDREN COME TO ME' — 99

Vera's story	100
The little girl who went home	105

... and other true stories

7   STRANGE LIGHTS AND OTHER MYSTERIES   107

The Mystery of the glowing cross	108
The light that hung in the air	111
The case of the lighted teddy bear	112
The Min-Min lights	113

8   THE MATTER OF EVIL   115

'Do not fear those who kill the body...'	116
The nurses' Ouija board	119
A Ouija board story from Scotland	120
Tarot cards	122

9   SOME ANIMAL STORIES   126

Do animals have souls?	127
A fleeting visit from Singh	141
Helen's story	143
A strange farewell story from Malaysia	145
The strange case of the neighing horse	146
A Mysterious photograph	148
The day Sheiba came back	148
The ghost cat of Manly manse	149
A husband, a wife, a boy and a dog	153
The man who delayed his own death	155

10   ALIENS, OR WHAT?   160

'Spaceships' (A poem)	161
The 'flying saucers' of Woomera	162
'How the moon gets back home'	162
That night at Mirrabooka	163

UFOs over Gloucester	165
The strange case of the Nullarbor lights	168
Something to think about	169
The Oakey UFO	170
'Angels or aliens'?	172
The lights of Dunedoo	174
UFO activity over Nowra	177

11 SOME MORE HEAD SCRATCHERS — 181

Be sure of your facts	182
The car that didn't break down	185
A story of betrayal	187
'Through each perplexing path of life'	188
Meg's story	191
The Dorrigo mountain spider	193

12 THE LIFE BEYOND THIS LIFE — 198

The final chapter	199
Stan's story	200
Marilyn's story	202
Hamish's story	205
Greg's story	207
Alora, the Swan	211
'A glimpse of eternity'	213

13 EPILOGUE — 220

... and other true stories

Have you read any of Lachlan's other books?

Some comments from readers

A Kangaroo Loose in Shetland: Excerpts from a Diary

Thank you so sincerely for the two copies of your wonderful book! What a beautiful experience, and it's wonderful that you could share it with us all, through your book.
M&D

Thank you for your book, which I found hard to put down. I was transported back to Shetland, to the land of puffins... and a beauty that is simply inspiring... I shall cherish these memories always.
Olive

...In Lachlan's charming account of his day to day adventures and encounters, you will see something of Shetland's remote and windswept beauty...the people of the North will become your friends, as they did for Lachlan and his wife Janet...
ES in "Span" magazine

A Kangaroo Loose in the Top Paddock

This book is one of those rare finds, a rich and genuine vein of homegrown Australian ecclesiastical humour, in the best tradition of Father Hartigan of "John O'Brien" fame.

The author has an obvious love for the wild Australian bush and the robust people who carve their living there... A Kangaroo Loose in the Top Paddock is an hilariously funny book from a writer of great literary talent... the publishers claim that at the end you will put this book down with a warm glow. I read it, and I did! ITC

... and other true stories

One Memorable Summer: A Scottish Adventure

I'm ordering three more of your book 'One Memorable Summer… I so enjoyed all your books and have become the designated orderer for St Davids.
Beth

I have just finished reading your One Memorable Summer in record time. I was unable to put it down.
Janette

Congratulations! What an entertaining and delightful read is your book.
Russ

I will be looking for this author's other books… "A Kangaroo Loose in the Top Paddock" and "A Kangaroo Loose in Shetland." Recommended.
"Insights" magazine

I was so disappointed when I got to the end. I kept wanting it to go on.
Netta

…almost like a sitcom in the style of Heartbeat, Doc Martin or the Vicar of Dibley. It is a highly readable, light and easy style and the Gaelic is almost always translated.
Rev Ivan Ransom

Mum can't wait to get into it. She has already read your other books a couple of times.
Daniel (who gave the book as a birthday gift for his mother)

www.akangarooloose.com

www.ingramcontent.com/pod-product-compliance
Lightning Source LLC
Chambersburg PA
CBHW070642160426
43194CB00009B/1549